PRAISE FOR LINDA HALE BUCKLIN

"If you have ever wondered if there is an afterlife, *The Distant Shore* will give you faith. This book will profoundly touch your heart, fill you with hope and joy, and encourage you to be more mindful in your daily life."

— SUSAN SMITH JONES, PHD

As Linda Bucklin's friend and co-author of *Come Rain or Come Shine: Friendships about Women*, I've been one of her life witnesses for 25 years. *The Distant Shore* carries us into her lifelong quest for a deeper understanding and experience of love. We celebrate Linda's successes, weep with compassion over her losses, and see our own lives differently as a result. Most of all, this book inspires us to reflect on our own connection to that distant shore.

— MARY KEIL

T0017525

THE DISTANT SHORE

THE DISTANT SHORE

STORIES OF LOVE AND FAITH IN THE AFTERLIFE

LINDA HALE BUCKLIN

Edited by Valerie Andrews

Cover Photo by John Bucklin

Book and cover design by eBook Prep
www.ebookprep.com

January, 2021
ISBN: 978-1-64457-222-1

ePublishing Works!
644 Shrewsbury Commons Ave
Ste 249
Shrewsbury PA 17361
United States of America

www.epublishingworks.com
Phone: 866-846-5123

TO MY BELOVED FAMILY

Song of the River

The snow melts on the mountain
And the water runs down to the spring,
And the spring in a turbulent fountain,
With a song of youth to sing
Runs down to the riotous river
And the river flows to the sea
And the water again
Goes back in rain
To the hills where it used to be.
And I wonder if life's deep mystery
Isn't much like the rain and the snow
Returning through all eternity
To the places it used to know...
So we shall run
The course begun
Till we reach the silent shore.
Then revisit earth
In a pure rebirth
From the heart of the virgin snow.
So don't ask why
We live or die,
Or whither, or when we go,
Or wonder about the mysteries
That only God may know.

—William Randolph Hearst

FOREWORD

BY SUSAN SMITH JONES, PHD

I first met Linda Bucklin through her book, *Beyond His Control: Memoir of a Disobedient Daughter,* and was so taken by her story of standing up to a powerful father that I tried to find a production company to make it into a movie. All true, it's a page-turner—a high society life of a prominent San Francisco family, world travels, a 10,000 acre ranch in Northern California, an important collection of Impressionist paintings, and the massive family fortune entirely left to her father's second wife.

Subsequently, I read Linda's heart-warming book, *The Love of Angels: Spiritual Encounters*. I also have been touched by angels, and two of my stories are included in this book.

Linda's latest book, *The Distant Shore*, will take you on an emotional journey that will profoundly touch your heart. When her husband Bill was alive, he resisted the possibility there might be something after death. But Linda got him to agree that were he to leave first, he would communicate his love to her in a way that she could recognize. She promised him she would do the same.

Bill remained true to his word, and Linda relates many instances after death where he reached out to her. "His guiding spirit continues to show me I am stronger than I think," Linda says, "and has also made me appreciate the beauty and wholeness of this life we are given. I am comforted, knowing there is life after death, and that Bill and I will be together again."

This book encourages us to be more mindful of our experience of living, to take inventory and assess what's essential and important and let go of the superfluous. Linda writes, "Now I pay more attention to the small moments when I visualize my wonderful family and dear friends, silently thanking them for their loving kindness, as I watch a hummingbird hover over blossoms on my lemon bush, dance to "Saturday Night Fever," read a poem by Mary Oliver, clip the ends of pale peach roses and arrange them with white freesias in my favorite glass vase, or thank God and all angels for their love and guidance."

I was impressed by Linda's willingness to learn and grow, to practice forgiveness and have faith in what her heart is telling her. In my book *Wired for High-Level Wellness: Simple Ways to Rejuvenate, Meditate & Prosper,* I echo this message: You have the power of love within you—it is the birthright and potential of every human being as a child of God. The only possible limitation is your own thought or belief. You, and only you, have the ability to create miracles in your life.

Linda shares her understanding of the afterlife: "There is no death, only a change of form from the physical to a rebirth into the life of the spirit. And from there our loved ones will help us as they did on earth. This knowledge that life continues after death has been a wonderful, healing tonic to ease my grief. The memories of Bill's life here, and the lives of all those who've touched my heart in love are never far from me."

There are really no coincidences, as you'll come to understand reading this book. Everything happens for a reason to teach us more about love, hope, and faith. I thank Linda for this wonderful book that I will refer to often.

INTRODUCTION

We've all lost people we've loved, and we've all dealt with our grieving in different ways. Bill, my beloved husband of 40 years, died unexpectedly after being ill for just one month. During our years together we had talked of our dying; we both hoped we wouldn't be a burden on each other or any of our loved ones. And we had made a pact that whoever passed first would communicate with the one who remained earthbound.

Throughout our marriage Bill's strong presence had reassured me, giving me a sense of safety I had not felt growing up. Helping me stand up to my abusive father, he saw my potential, urged me to believe in myself and go for my dreams. For every small success I would achieve, he was thrilled.

Weak and in great pain at the end of his life, he knew he could no longer be that strong, sturdy guy who had always been my protector and advocate; he also knew were he to live, he would be in a greatly diminished state. As shocked and devastated as I was that Bill died so quickly, I came to accept that his not lingering was his final earthly gift to me. Difficult as that was for us all, I finally understood it was intentional. However, he has honored our agreement, coming to me mainly in dreams and through music.

From the afterlife, Bill's guiding spirit continues to show me I am stronger than I think and has also made me appreciate more deeply the beauty and the wholeness of this life we are given. In keeping an open mind and an open heart, I find unexpected riches everywhere, in my family, my friends, in nature, in my dreams. And I am comforted, knowing that there is life after death, and that Bill and I will be together again.

Linda Hale Bucklin
November 2020

THE MESSAGE

PART I

A MOMENT OF GRACE

Loving his red wine and grilled duck, my husband Bill always looked forward to a cocktail (or two) and a good meal. In early February 2016, I noticed he'd lost his usual enthusiasm for lunch or dinner; worried, I suggested he get a physical. Stubborn and wary of most doctors (his grandmother being a good friend of Mary Baker Eddy), he resisted and resisted until I finally prevailed. Our appointment was February 14. On March 16 Bill died.

During that month's time, Bill went downhill quickly, but I was so preoccupied with his getting better I never faced the possibility he might die. Diagnosed with pneumonia in his left lung, he was given a weeklong prescription of antibiotics and told by his doctor to call if there were any problems. Soon thereafter he was hospitalized for five days, released and then readmitted only a week later.

Though I didn't understand Bill was dying, I saw he was no

longer my big, tough guy who had always seemed invincible. He was now hooked up to IV's for fluids, for antibiotics, for pain meds; I could hardly weave my way through the dangling tubes to hold his hand and put my head on his chest. Nurses came in and out, a breathing specialist gave him a powerful inhaler, a speech therapist came to see if he could swallow enough to handle soft food. (He couldn't, and later a hospice nurse told me that when this happens, it is a sign the patient is dying.)

During this time, there was a moment of grace, one that I hold with the greatest of care. Nick, my youngest son, had relieved me for a spell, but upon my return, Bill smiled, and his eyes lit up. "Oh Linda, I have been remembering our life together, all those wonderful times we've had, how happy you've made me." I hugged him for a long time and told him he was the only one for me, that I loved him with all my heart. We were both crying.

And then he said, "I want you to be perfectly honest with me," and I waited for what else he was going to say, but then a nurse bustled in to check his vital signs, and that moment was forever lost. I wonder still what he was going to ask me—perhaps did I know if he were dying—and at that point, I didn't and hadn't let myself get anywhere near that possibility. A day later the doctor ordered more transfusions.

Bill could hardly move; frustrated, one night he ripped out all the tubes. He just wanted to go home, but I still believed he would make it. The next morning the doctor came by. Surprised to see her so early, I asked, "Can you give me an update on Bill's progress?" "Mrs. Bucklin," she said, "The blood transfusions aren't working." My heart tumbling, I said, "So what is our next step?" Looking me squarely in the eye, she answered, "That means there is a time frame."

While my mind heard those seven words, my heart, suspended in the silence that surrounded us, didn't process them. I could hardly breathe, a tangled mass of feelings piercing my insides. On a distant level I understood that Bill was leaving this earth, but I wasn't able to accept this reality. Surrounding me with their strong arms, my three sons realized I was paralyzed emotionally and took charge. That afternoon Bill and I came home by ambulance to be with family and our two Labradors.

That was on Friday, March 11. Bill was conscious and so happy to see Meg, his loyal, loving Lab, who promptly lay down by his bed, always on watch for her master. My kind neighbors had set up an oxygen tank and hospital bed next to ours. Hospice came by and instructed me on how to administer the morphine. Surrounded by family, Bill told us how lucky and beloved he felt, and how much he loved us. He reached out his hand, no longer warm, to grasp mine and smiled. "Oh, Linda," he said. "Oh, Linda."

There were so many things I wanted to say to him just one more time—how I loved his sense of humor, how I was forever grateful for his standing by my side, how thrilled I was we shared a deep love of the outdoors, how much I loved him, how I didn't know if I could still keep on living without him, how he was my guy no matter what. One more time I wanted to feel his strong clasp and look into his beautiful hazel eyes and know he understood.

Holding his hand and telling him I loved him, I watched as he slipped in and out of consciousness. The next day he had moved to a different level, no longer able to talk or physically respond in any way. I lay next to him for five more days. On March 16 Nick and I were with him when the hospice nurse arrived. I asked her how long she felt he had left, and after checking his vital signs, she said, "He's strong; he might have a few more days."

After she had gone, Nick left to do a few quick errands. I sat next to Bill and stroked his arm. I told him how I loved lying next to him in our sleeping bags in Montana, waiting for the Evening Star to emerge; how happy I'd been sitting next to him while we watched hundreds of mallard and widgeon, framed by the scarlet sunset beyond the Buttes, take off from Gun Dog Lake, both of us awed by the beauty of their flight. I told him his unconditional love and sense of humor carried me through my darkest times. I told him I was the luckiest girl in the world to be his wife. "You are my beloved," I said.

Suddenly his breathing changed. It grew more rapid. He took in one more breath, a mere whisper, and then it became part of the air around him. His body was still, and he was gone.

ALWAYS ON MY MIND

O n our long road trips to Montana and Marysville, California, I would read Bill excerpts from books about the afterlife, in hopes I might convince him to share my belief that our spirit lives on after we leave our physical bodies here on earth. I started with *Letters from the Light*, an afterlife journal as described by deceased Judge David Hatch and written through the hand of Elsa Barker.

Elsa Barker writes in her introduction, "The effect of these letters on me personally has been to remove entirely any fear of death which I may ever have had, to strengthen my belief in immortality, to make life beyond the grave as real and vital as the life here in the sunshine."

As I read Bill various letters of Judge Hatch, I could tell he was interested, but still resisting the possibility there might be something after we died. I continued to share other books —*Appointments with Heaven*, by Reggie Anderson, *To Heaven and Back* by Mary C. Neal, and *Proof of Heaven,* Eben Alexander—all written by doctors who had been skeptical about life after death until they had their own experiences to convince them otherwise. Bill never told me to stop reading, but he was non-committal in his comments. I did get him to agree that if he were to leave first, he would communicate his love to me in a way that I would recognize. I promised him I would do the same.

Bill loved and found solace in nature. Often, we voiced our wonder of the sight of a full moon peeking above the hills of Stinson, rising heavily until it pushed free of the horizon, a perfect circle in the dark sky. On nights with a new moon, we would walk to the end of the beach to find our favorite constellation, the Pleiades. I know Bill carried within him deep currents of spiritual yearning that he found easiest to express through the beauty he saw in all places wild.

I have always believed in God and angels, in reincarnation, and life after death. Raised in the Episcopal tradition, I searched for answers to my yearning to understand what might lie beyond this life on earth. In my early teens, I read Edgar Cayce's books and was drawn to his stories of our living many lives. But in my family of origin, no one ever discussed religion or spiritual levels of existence.

Soon after my mother died, one of her closest friends sent me a small book, *Forever* by Mildred Crum, with the following letter enclosed:

Dear Linda,
Your mother gave me this beautiful book as a baby present when
my first son, Tom, was born. I would now like you to have it.
Always my love, Eileen.

The first chapter opened, "They met—Colin and Julie—not
very long before they were born," and my hands began to shake.
After I had finished it, I couldn't stop crying. It was the story
about two souls in heaven who fall in love, then have to leave
each other to be born on earth. Colin is called first, and Julie
worries about how they will ever find each other again. Colin
promises they will meet in 27 years in the same place. He reas-
sures her they are destined to be together on the Other Side.

My mother never once spoke of her belief in reincarnation
and life after death, but I understood then I had intuited her feelings about life after death from an early age. And I did hear her
often say with great love that she and Dad were "meant to be."
"Destined," she would add softly. After her heartbreak over the
unraveling of her marriage and her subsequent violent death, I
sometimes wondered if Mom were waiting for Dad when he
passed over 27 years later. Remembering her loving heart and
kind ways, I suspect she was, her arms open wide and her brown
eyes alight with love.

When Bill passed, I, like Julie, worried about how we would
ever find each other. I worried I'd never hear from him again.
But one morning I did. After checking my email on my iPhone, I
put it on the counter, stood up, called to my dog Sage and started
walking into the other room. Then out from my phone came

Willie Nelson's voice singing "You Are Always on My Mind." Stunned, I turned around to listen.

Maybe I didn't hold you all those lonely, lonely times
I guess I never told you I'm so happy that you were mine.
Tell me, tell me that your sweet love hasn't died
Give me one more chance to keep you satisfied.
You were always on my mind.

I knew immediately it was Bill communicating with me. He'd chosen Willie Nelson, an outdoors guy his age, and a song we liked, to tell me of his love for me in ways specific to our relationship. Weeping and grateful, I called my three sons and told them Bill had found me. Since then he's picked many times to communicate, through words, dreams, and music.

One bluebird windless day at Stinson Beach, with temperatures in the 80's, I decided to take Sage for a walk. Heading towards the channel that runs between Bolinas and Stinson, we wended our way along the path above the water until we reached the end of the sand spit. It was low tide.

I found myself standing right next to a large washed up fish, one I'd never seen before in my 40 years of combing the beach. I immediately thought, "Oh, Bill would have been so interested in this!" Deciding I would take a picture so I could ask my son John what it was, I realized I didn't have my iPhone with me. Despite the suffocating heat, I walked a long 10 minutes back to the house to get it. By then I was hot and sweaty but determined to document this fish before it was washed away.

Putting my phone in my shorts, I retraced my steps. As I

stood there looking down at the fish, suddenly music came from my back pocket. "Hey there, you with the stars in your eyes" rang out. Then the music stopped, but I knew absolutely it was Bill calling to me. I stood still, silent, waiting, my heart open, and then three songs followed, all favorites of Bill's and mine —"People Will Say We're in Love" from *Oklahoma*, "All I Ask of You" from *Phantom of the Opera*, and ending with "We Are Family." And then just as suddenly as the music started, it stopped.

Throughout all this I hadn't touched my phone, but I understood clearly that Bill was once again using it as the conduit to communicate with me from the other side—to reassure me of his love and let me know he was watching out for me. Filled with yearning, I felt strong and joyful, and at the same time so vulnerable and weak that a feather could have knocked me over.

I took many pictures of the fish to show John, who correctly identified it as a thresher shark, a species not common to the area. I often return to the memory of that afternoon, comforted, feeling that Bill is happy and nearby.

That night, Bill came to me in a dream. "How will you find me?" I asked him anxiously. The unbearable thought that we might never be together again tore through me like a riptide, but then he said, "Linda, don't worry. I will find you." I felt his strong hands clasp mine. When I awakened, my hands, normally ice cold, were warm and tingly. I held onto this dream that eased my aching heart.

A few weeks later, I had a recurring dream in which Bill was still alive. I saw him in a crowd and called out excitedly. When I finally reached his side, I begged him to come home with me.

But he was reluctant, saying, "No, I've met another woman." There was no changing his mind. I awakened devastated by his words and the thought of losing him again. Later I had a session with an Intuitive who helped me understand the meaning of this dream.

Crying, I told her that in life, Bill would never leave me and that we had agreed to communicate with one another after death. After listening quietly, she said," Linda, a good part of your life story has been about loss and betrayal. Bill, who would never betray you, is leading you toward a higher level of forgiveness in this dream. He is telling you it's time to deal with the other people who have left you, then move forward. He wants you to take this big spiritual step."

She continued, "Trust your agreement. He will be waiting for you when you pass over. Remember, you are always in a state of union. Together you have created a contract of abiding love. Nothing can break this."

RESCUE ME

One Saturday morning I drove home from Stinson Beach. All the way over the hill, I played my favorite CD's from the 50's and 60's, oldies but goodies. Suddenly a memory came to mind. It was years ago, and Bill and I were driving to the duck club. I turned on the radio and much to my surprise I heard the Chords singing their hit, "Sh-Boom," one of my favorite oldies, a song of innocence and yearning, of perfect love with a touch of lust. I sang along.

"Sh-Boom" begins with the words Life could be a dream, and then a tenor voice adds:

If I could take you up in paradise up above
If you would tell me I'm the only one you love
If you would let me spend my whole life loving you...
Life could be a dream, sweetheart.

As a 10-year-old hearing this song for the first time, I was happy and wanted to get up to dance. What fun it was to imagine falling in love with someone who would spend his entire life loving me!

As I reminisced, Bill laughed and said, "Give me Puccini any day of the week." Then the memory faded, and I was back alone in my car.

Driving into Mill Valley, I ejected my CD and turned the radio to 560, a station I often listen to for news and tips on investing, financial planning and real estate. Never had I heard any musical segments. An ad for MacDonald Real Estate was abruptly interrupted by Bill's and my favorite aria from *La Boheme*, with Rodolfo singing of his great love for Mimi. Stunned, I pulled over. I couldn't believe what I was hearing. And then I realized—without a doubt—it was Bill once again conveying his love to me, using music as his vehicle. Feeling his presence, I listened to this beautiful aria. Then just as suddenly as it burst onto the station, the music ended, and a voice came back on the air, opining about Marin County real estate.

Recently I had a down day, two disappointments in my social life, nothing major but enough to sink my spirits. I felt a current of sadness in my heart, reminding me how much I missed Bill. When he was alive, I could always share my hurts and joys with him. That morning I had coffee and was sitting quietly, still feeling blue. I wanted to call a close friend but couldn't find my phone.

Suddenly I heard music coming from my study and remembered that I'd left my phone on my desk the night before. I thought I had turned it off. Rushing in, I heard the song "Rescue Me" by Fontella Bass:

Rescue me, take me in your arms
Rescue me, I want your tender charms
I am lonely and I am blue
I need you and your love, too.
Come on and take my heart
Take our love and comfort every part.

I couldn't believe what I was hearing. While Bill didn't share my love of oldies, he knew I was crazy about this song and clearly chose it to get my attention and tell me he was aware I was feeling lonely. I sensed his presence and knew he was trying to cheer me up. As soon as that song ended, "Be My Baby," by the Ronettes came on, and this was his answer, reassuring me of his love.

The night we met I knew I needed you so
And if I had the chance, I'd never let you go
So won't you please be, be my baby?
For every kiss you give me, I'll give you three
Oh, since the day I saw you
I have been waiting for you
You know I will adore you 'til eternity.

Then suddenly the music stopped. While some might look for a rational explanation, I know it was Bill once again comforting me.

USIC PRESIDENT'S CUP

The International Tennis Club of the United States of America was formed to promote good fellowship among tennis players and encourage the highest standard of sportsmanship among players of all nations. Active members must be accomplished ones, who have represented their country in international competition or won national championships in any age category.

The seventh USIC President's Cup, hosted by the French, took place in Normandy in September 2018. I was invited to be part of Team USA. On the one hand thrilled and honored, I also felt uneasy about traveling alone, and insecure about my physical level of my recovery from a bad fall ten months earlier. Was I brave enough, was I fit enough, to accept this incredible invitation? I couldn't decide.

The deadline to accept or decline looming, my *no* voice was winning. And then I had the great fortune to run into Andrea

Barnes, who mentioned she was on the team and strongly encouraged me to come. We could meet in Paris, she suggested, and then travel together to Normandy and back. I took a deep breath, and suddenly words I didn't know I was going to say tumbled out. "OK, yes, yes. I'll go."

Forever grateful for her support, I count Andrea as one of the angels who guided me to participate in this unforgettable event. Celeste, our Paris angel, helped us with logistics. And fellow teammate Bruce and his beautiful wife Jodi, two more angels, drove Andrea and me everywhere, including from Paris to Normandy where we met the rest of our team.

The day before our competition began, both teams boarded a bus to go to Omaha Beach, where the American 1st and 29th Infantry Divisions, suffering heavy losses, had landed on June 6, 1944. We also visited the Normandy American Cemetery, which honors the 9,387 soldiers who died during that battle. As I walked through the perfectly aligned headstones and read name after name of these courageous men, many barely 19, who gave their lives for America, France and freedom for the Western world, I couldn't stop my tears. Kneeling, humbled by their ultimate sacrifices, I silently prayed my thanks.

The next day our matches began, and again I felt as if angels were watching over me. After being spanked badly in singles, only winning one game off my opponent and feeling quite discouraged, I teamed up with Andrea for the ladies doubles and Jeff for mixed—fantastic partners who encouraged me all the way—which resulted in two wins for our team. Final result: Team USA won 19 matches to 12 for France.

That last evening in Paris, Andrea and I had dinner and then went to our room to pack for our early departure the next morning. Clothes on the floor, thyroid pills in the bathroom, tennis racquets off in the corner, cell phone about to run out of power, I was feeling very scattered. "First things, first," I said to myself. Attaching my converter to my cell phone, I plugged it into a socket near my bed. Suddenly all the lights went out in our room.

Unplugging my phone, I found its flashlight so I could see to push the button for the front desk. Then I placed it on the table next to my bed. Nervously I explained our situation to the manager, saying it was important to get the lights back on as soon as possible. Since it was a Sunday night, she explained, it might be a while before she could get someone there to rectify the situation.

As I sat on my bed in the dark, my heart pounding, my stomach in knots, suddenly I heard music coming from my phone which was across the room. It was Cliff Richard singing "All I Ask of You," a favorite song of Bill's and mine. The first words were:

No more talk of darkness
Forget these wide-eyed fears.
I'm here, nothing can harm you.
My words will warm and calm you.

Anywhere you go, let me go too.
That's all I ask of you.

As I listened to this familiar song, so appropriate to my situation, I knew without a doubt this was Bill, once again using music we both love to communicate. Reassuring me that all would be well, he reminded me he is still watching out for me. I immediately settled down. A few minutes after the song had ended, the handyman knocked on the door, and soon thereafter the lights came on.

I will always remember this amazing trip to beautiful Normandy—the wonderful people, competitive tennis, delicious meals, and our special time at Omaha Beach. Mixed in with these indelible memories is one of Bill, who was there, too, celebrating us, never far from my side.

MY CANADIAN CLUB GUY

Forty-three years ago, close friends invited Bill and me to visit them in the British Virgin Islands. Great swimming! Amazing snorkeling! Boat trips! Bill, who grew up near Oceanside, California where he spent many hours in or on the ocean, was very much at home in the water. I, on the other hand, get seasick easily, and am a lousy swimmer. I once almost drowned bodysurfing at Makapu, leaving me with a great respect, bordering on terror, of the ocean.

Since Bill was excited to go, I jumped on his wagon. Not yet married, we were still in the getting-to-know each other, crazy-in-love stage. I was not ready to own up to any of my weaknesses. After we arrived, our hosts showed us to our room and then discreetly left us on our own. As we looked out at panoramic views of a wide, uninhabited beach on one side and steep cliffs running down to the open ocean on the other, Bill suggested we go to the beach and snorkel.

Grabbing towels, a bottle of wine, and some sandwiches—with little thought of why no one else was enjoying this beautiful beach—we clamored down the narrow path to the shimmering white sands below. Laying out our towels, we couldn't believe our good luck that we were alone. Wanting to impress Bill with my snorkeling prowess (ha!), I got up and ran into the water. I heard Bill soon splash in behind me.

Adjusting my snorkel, I began swimming out from the beach to where I could see some submerged rocks. A few colorful fish darted off, but as I swam into deeper water, four sizable fish began slowly swimming towards me. Even though I had only seen barracuda in pictures, when the biggest one came closer, I knew what it was. I panicked; I couldn't control my breathing, my mask fogged up, and I started kicking wildly. Right at that moment, Bill swam in front of me, shielding me, and the fish reluctantly turned away.

We both swam quickly to shore. "Wow," I said. "That wasn't a lot of fun. Now I see why no one else is here." Always quick to see the humor in a situation, Bill, wearing his signature red madras trunks, flexed his arm muscles, strutted around, and said, "I need a Canadian Club," referring to the current popular ad about macho outdoors men choosing this as their drink of choice. Laughing, we opened our wine, and I toasted to my newfound protector. As we later related our adventure to our hosts, they said apologetically, "Oh goodness, we forgot to tell you that no one ever swims on that beach! Too many barracuda!"

Throughout our marriage Bill indeed became my strongest advocate and protector. Recently, when I was at a low point, wondering if I could keep finding strength to carry on, I took my dog Sage for a walk on the beach at Stinson. I just happened to notice a large, long fish with sharp teeth and big eyes, one I have never seen over 40 years of walking this beach, struggling to get back into the ocean. Immediately I knew it was a barracuda (an unusual sight on any Northern California beach), and at the same moment I remembered Bill's and my time so many years ago when we were—for a few long minutes—swimming among them.

Once again, I felt Bill there, nearby, reassuring me that even though he is physically no longer on earth, he is still my big, strong Canadian Club guy watching over me, reminding me of his enduring love.

SAYING GOODBYE

Christian, John, Nick and I decided to meet in our Montana camp to scatter Bill's ashes. John was the first to arrive. As he rounded the last bend of the road leading to our tents, he saw Bill sitting in his favorite spot on the porch, binoculars around his neck, a book in his hand, Meg by his feet. As he drove closer, the image faded.

He then felt Bill's spirit surrounding him, and he couldn't stop crying. Everywhere he walked, to the edge of the North Fork, to the top of the hill where evenings we would all meet for drinks, he knew Bill was nearby. Christian, Nick and I arrived soon thereafter; we stood with our arms entwined, silent, absorbing the pain of Bill's absence and remembering his presence. Montana, this camp, was where he was his happiest. We spent four bluebird days there.

On the third evening we hiked to the top of the property and

sat on benches John had made from wood from the old home-
steader's cabin. We each took a turn spreading Bill's ashes.
When it was Nick's turn, he said, "Dad, this morning, Christian,
John and I fished the North Fork at the southern edge of the Bob
Marshalls. This is one of our favorite pieces of water, and we
wouldn't know it if it weren't for you. Do you remember how the
mountains rise above forests scorched by wildfires to the north,
and how the big Blackfoot to the south winds its way to meet the
North Fork? We fished in your honor, Dad, and we used the dry
flies you recommended. And guess what? We all caught some
great fish, even Christian!" Laughing, Christian raised his glass
and toasted "Bourbon Bill."

I hadn't fished the entire time. But on the last day, I decided
to walk down to the river to try my luck. As I stood looking
across crystal clear waters, I was unsure of where to put my fly.
Usually I would cast from the bank, but that day, uncharacteristi-
cally, I was drawn to a spot towards the middle of the river. "I
can do this," I thought, wading out cautiously to where the
current was strong.

As I raised my arm to cast, I suddenly felt Bill's steady hand
guiding mine, and my fly landed—much to my surprise—exactly
where I wanted it to be. Immediately the water moved, and an
aggressive cutthroat grabbed my fly. When I landed it, I was
amazed: It was by far the largest trout I had ever caught on this
river. After its release, I waded back to the bank and sat in awe,
understanding Bill once again was letting me know he was
nearby, watching over me, thrilled to have had a hand in this
recent success.

I haven't been back to our camp again, but when I do return, I will walk down to the river. I will wade out to deeper waters and cast to that spot where another hungry trout might lie. And I will remember.

DUCK HUNTING WITH JIMMY

For many years Bill and I belonged to a beautiful duck club in Northern California, where we shot first with Shadow, then Meg, and finally Sage, our three beloved Labs. John and Nick learned to shoot with us in the flooded rice fields and wild oak trees where wood ducks swooped and weaved. I learned to call in the mallard, yet what I loved most was sitting next to Bill in the blind and watching our dog work her retrieving magic.

After Bill died, we kept our membership for another season before admitting our duck hunting days without Bill, reminders too painful for us to handle, were over. On our last hunt on a bluebird day, with the Buttes clearly outlined in the morning light, Sage made an amazing final retrieve of a drake mallard John had shot. After that we retired our guns with heavy hearts.

Jimmy, one of Bill's closest friends, recently invited John, Sage and me hunting, our first time since we had left our club. As I was unpacking my bag, I noticed on the wall above my bed a collage of photos of Bill, Jimmy and me from our hunts together in years past. "Look," I said to John, "there's your Dad."

It was drizzling when we walked in darkness out to our blind early the next morning, Sage far ahead on the rice check, already on the lookout for ducks. As we settled down in our barrels, the rain stopped, and we saw a glimmer of light on the eastern horizon. An occasional duck flew over, but the shooting was slow. And then, as the sun began to rise, we saw a huge rainbow. That moment scores of widgeon poured through it toward our blind. My heart ached that Bill wasn't here to see this.

We had a glorious shoot, and Sage didn't miss a retrieve. Later that morning after our goodbyes, John, Sage and I headed back to Marin. As we were driving on Highway 37, the route Bill always took on our way home from hunting, John turned on the radio. Suddenly we heard the start of Rachmaninoff's Second Piano Concerto in C minor, Bill's favorite piece. John and I listened in silence, tears running down our cheeks.

When that finished, immediately Chopin's Nocturne for Piano, Opus 9, Bill's second favorite, followed. It was then I understood Bill was letting us know he'd been there with us, watching the sun rise over the flooded rice fields, thrilled that we had had such a wonderful shoot, and mightily impressed that Sage, just an inexperienced hunter when Bill died, had performed so well.

Postscript: I sent this story to Jimmy for his approval and he was glad to be included in the book. Less than two months later, in Jackson Hole, after skiing 7,736 vertical feet with two of his daughters and various grandchildren, Jimmy died of a cardiac arrest. An outgoing, larger-than-life cowboy, he was beloved by many. For Jimmy, family came first, then friends, followed closely by his love of hunting, fishing, skiing, horseback riding, hiking, and all creatures wild.

Lisa, his oldest daughter who lives in Jackson Hole, told me of their animated nature discussions. There were sightings of moose in his flower bed, a coyote crossing his bridge, a fox returning with dinner for her pups, fish rising in Fish Creek, or the herd of elk that blended into the aspen grove above his porch. Jimmy also loved birds, especially eagles.

The morning after his death, Lisa and her sister Christina were driving towards their parents' house when they sighted an eagle—by no means an everyday occurrence. It was perched in a tall pine tree. Then it flew towards Jimmy's bridge, hovering over five white swans that had gathered in the river below.

The wildlife show continued. As they headed up the driveway to the house, they saw his favorite elk herd also in the river. In an unusually joyful and carefree way, the eagle suddenly swooped down toward them, then dove over the herd. Moments later, a flock of ducks landed. Jimmy's daughters knew then without a doubt their father was there, saying goodbye, reminding them in his own way, that he will always be nearby.

In a recent session with an Intuitive, I asked about Jimmy. She said, "Yes, he's with your husband. They are in a beautiful grassy area, and there are lots of ducks and geese around. They are laughing and teasing each other. I see Jimmy died from heart problems. He wished he could have had more time here. He is showing me his great love for his family."

HEALING & FORGIVENESS

PART II

MEYER LEMONS

The present and the past exist together in our hearts, and any small thing can carry us either way, a song, a fragrance, a photograph, a book marked to a certain page. Here in Mill Valley, the window of my study overlooks a hardy Meyer lemon bush. It's January and cold enough to put frost on my car windows. Yet this small tree is overflowing with fruit. When I pick a lemon and cut it open, I inhale its sweet, spicy scent and am drawn back to memories of the HE Ranch, the ranch of my youth.

Lost to me over 50 years ago, it was the place from my past I loved best. In reading photographer Sally Mann's autobiography, I came across a word I'd never seen before—*hiraeth*—which she uses to describe her love of her family's farm in Virginia. It is a Welsh term for loving a place, for having a near umbilical attachment to it, for homesickness tinged with yearning. It describes perfectly how I feel for the ranch.

I first went there when I was two, my brother Rusty, five, and Hilary, my sister, six. They got to bunk on the sleeping porch, a long, screened-in area with beds lined up military-style and a view of Sulphur Creek in the distance. I happily slept with my beloved nurse Frances in a small room nearby, lulled to sleep by their whispers and muffled laughter.

I remember walking through the rows of corn, their stalks shading me from the relentless heat and hiding me from the rest of the world. Frances, however, always knew where I was. She'd grab my hand and lead me towards the rope swing hanging from a branch of the big black oak tree near the corrals. There, she'd push me, high, higher, until I thought my toes were touching the sky.

When we moved up to the big adobe house my parents built, we left behind the bantam hens, the corn and tomatoes picked fresh for dinner. We stopped swimming in Sulphur Creek and forgot about the rope swing that overlooked stalls that housed Flicka, my mother's young mare, and Diablo, my father's fiery stallion. We dove instead into our new swimming pool and raced through gardens filled with hollyhock, iris, hydrangea, and roses. We picked Meyer lemons from the prickly green bushes and drank lemonade made from their juice.

As I look out at my Mill Valley Meyer lemons, these memories and many more tumble through me: Golden California hills, black oaks, hum of crickets, frogs singing their nighttime chorus, little streams lined with bay, springs circled with watercress, the North Star shining brightly in a starry sky, charades, dominoes, panty raids, croquet battles, horseback rides home in the dark, coyotes yipping their hunting call, hours sitting around a long dining room table, all of us laughing.

I took my mother's hand and walked out to the porch. My father, sister, and two brothers joined us. We watched the full moon rise slowly into the black sky illuminating the landscape for miles. No one said a word. We were together then, the six of us, our hands joined, and our loyalty pledged. We were a team, a family, inviolate, invincible, loving each other and the ranch with all our hearts.

Filled with *hireath*, I stop with this memory, willing myself not to go further. How could any one of us then ever have imagined what would happen to this family of ours just a short while later? Had I known that soon I would never be able to return to the ranch, would I have been strong enough to bear this heartbreak? I'm not sure.

Had I known that for 16 long years my father would forbid my siblings to contact me except through attorneys, without Bill would have I believed in myself enough to endure? I am not sure. Since Dad died, over two decades ago, the four of us have gotten together on a few occasions, but it's never been the same.

I pray we can somehow, someday, put back the pieces of what remains, these memories serving as a reminder of our joyful, innocent love for each other and the ranch. Although we have traveled far from these halcyon days, I still believe we will come together again and delight in the magic of a full moon rising above the horizon of distant hills to illuminate the beauty of a wild landscape below.

HE HUNG THE MOON

R ecently I found some old Kodak slides of pictures my
father took 55 years ago up at the ranch. When I hold
one up to the light, I see my mother, 51, just six years before she
dies, her short hair a riot of shiny red curls that frame her heart-
shaped face. She is looking directly at the camera and smiling.
There high on her left cheek is her brown beauty mark.

Wearing a faded blue work shirt, she holds her Browning 20-
gauge shotgun. I figure she has just returned from a wild pigeon
shoot with Dad. Hap, my younger brother, 12 years old at the
time, is also there, standing slightly behind her, a wide smile on
his face. They both look relaxed and seem happy Dad is taking
their picture.

Later I know they will feast on their bounty that Dad has
barbecued, making sure to marinate the birds with his sauce. (I
still use it, and always someone will comment on how delicious
it is.) "It's Dad's secret sauce," I say, "a recipe we guard closely."

After much pleading, I part with its ingredients—lemon juice, butter, and Worcestershire sauce—and everyone laughs when they hear how simple it is.

Two months before, Dad had taken all of us on an unforgettable, amazing trip to Mozambique, where we camped and hunted for a month in open jeeps or on foot with our white hunters as guides. A trip filled with adventure, beautiful wild rivers and plains, it also was irreplaceably special: the last trip our entire family ever took together. I hold close to my heart memories of our sitting around the campfire, playing pranks, looking up at the star-studded black African night sky, moving closer together when we heard the lions roar, feeling as if we were an unbreakable team, a family that would stay together forever.

A year later Dad took Mom, always the great sport, on a physically arduous trip to India to bag a tiger. I saw pictures of them, sitting high in box-like seats astride elephants and in the jungle at various stands, and heard their tales of Dad shooting a trophy one. Mom got ill from an unknown virus and almost died. But both they and the tiger skin finally made it back to San Francisco. Gaining the 12 pounds she had lost, Mom recovered her happy spirit and was ready the next year to accompany Dad, Hap and me, to Kenya. There we each shot an elephant, and it was then I retired my rifle. Mom did as well.

When we were young, Dad was full of tricks and fun ideas of how to spend our leisure time. In San Francisco one very foggy night, unknown to us, he tied a thin string to the edge of the heavy damask curtains in our large living room and then held the other end in his hand, the string invisible to our young eyes.

Gathering us together in front of the fire, he started telling stories about the Hoodeladoons, small creatures who live in the fog. He started 'hoo, hooing' them, and suddenly the curtain moved. Hilary screamed and ran out of the room. I grabbed Rusty's hand, and then Dad started to laugh.

Deemed too young for certain of his pranks, I remember watching him and Rusty (on a ladder) place in a corner a bucket full of water propped up by a broom. Dad then called Hilary to come help him hold the handle. When she did, he immediately walked away, leaving her alone, gripping tightly to the handle to keep the bucket balanced from falling. Finally, she gave up and was drenched.

Another time Dad was driving Mom, Hilary, aged eight, and me, aged four, up to his duck club near the Marysville Buttes. It was dark, we were nowhere near any sign of civilization and the girls needed to go to the bathroom. Dad drove off into a large field, and we tumbled out. Always the lady, Mom looked for cover and found none. So she said, "Girls, your father is looking the other way; let's just pull down our pants and go." He waited for the perfect moment and then turned on the headlights to capture three lily-white bare bottoms. We all shrieked.

Once I found in a joke store a plastic ice cube with a big bluebottle fly in its center. Thrilled I bought it and used it at the first available opportunity—one of Mom's incredible lunches at the ranch, where 16 of us, family and friends, were seated at the long rectangular table. I had snuck it into Dad's water glass with other real ice cubes. As Adrian, our butler, was passing a large platter filled with cold chicken, roast beef, ham, avocado and heirloom tomatoes with basil, I could hardly contain myself. I saw Dad take a long swig from his glass and set it down.

Mrs. Metcalf, his luncheon partner, just happened to be watching and said, "Prentis, I think there might be a fly in your water!" Furious, Dad saw the fly and angrily called for Adrian to come immediately. I realized I needed to fess up quickly which I did. Bemused, Mom looked at me and said, "Now we're cooking with gas!" And all of us except Dad joined in her laughter. I understood then that while Dad loved playing jokes on everyone else, he really didn't appreciate it when the joke was on him.

At the ranch Dad was the organizer extraordinaire. He planned charades, croquet, backgammon, domino, and ping-pong tournaments, and best of all our annual hare and hound hunt, a game we played on horseback. There were two teams (I was always on Dad's team), and the objective was simple. One team, the hares, given a half hour head start, tied ribbons on trees, bushes, fences, looking for the most difficult places we could, to leave the faintest trail as possible. The other team, the hounds, then started off in our pursuit, collecting the ribbons as they hunted us.

Dad told Lizzie, my best friend, and me to ride off in another direction and make a false trail. We did and then galloped back to catch up with the rest of the group. He led our team, finally, to the shade of Fraser Creek where we hid the horses behind a grove of bay trees and sat down to wait. Drifting off under a thick blanket of heat, I was startled awake by the sound of horses crashing through the manzanita above us. I saw Mom riding her mare Dune down the steep banks with her team behind, and I was happy we were found.

We caught fresh trout for dinner, and when it grew dark, a full moon rose up over the Geysers. We saddled up and headed for home and my horse, Tickle, the fastest of them all, kept up with my father. Galloping in and out of the shadows the moon cast through the live oak trees, from above we must have looked like a band of coyotes streaking through the night.

My older sister, Hilary, has wonderful pictures of Mom when she is young. In one taken during the World War II, they both are dressed in nurse's uniforms, Mom's for her work for the Red Cross, and Hilary's for her make-believe. They are holding hands, and Mom is looking down at her with love. There are others taken at Aptos, San Francisco, the ranch. Except for the formal album I have of my first wedding, I have only two pictures of me with Mom, both taken in Mozambique. In one she and I are sitting in the jeep ready to take off for a day of hunting with Wally, our guide, and in another we are kneeling next to the cape buffalo Mom shot. All others are the images I carry in my mind and heart.

My first complete memory of being alone with Mom after Frances left was when I was six. She invited me to accompany her on an errand in downtown San Francisco. Going on streets I'd never seen before, I was astonished at how well she found her way to her destination. After she'd parked, crossing Sutter Street, she took my hand, and we went into Paul Elder's, her favorite bookstore. Walking on the uneven wood floors and looking at rows and rows of books, I felt happy and important, especially when Mom let me pick out a book—*Old Mother West Wind* by

Thornton W. Burgess. The clerk wrapped it and even tied a bow on top. I saved the paper and ribbon, putting them in the corner of my dresser, reminders of my special outing.

I loved going anywhere with her, whether it was to Swan Oyster Depot where we sat, side by side, on high, wire-backed seats and savored a shrimp or crab cocktail, and then afterwards, across California Street to Blum's, where Mom would always buy me a cinnamon bar. Or we would go Paul's Flower Shop, a small hole-in-the-wall store with the best flowers in town. Aside from roses, spring flowers were our favorites: peonies, hyacinth, lilac, lily of the valley, tuberose, and narcissus. She always let me select some flowers of my own that I would arrange, carefully trying to mimic her creations, and then I would place it on her bedside table next to her books.

A friendly presence, she never raised her voice or got cross with me, but somehow I knew I was a disappointment. Shopping for clothes was a challenge; by the time I was 10, I would take the bus downtown and head for Lanz, known for its colorful, lively Austrian fabrics, where I was permitted to pick out a dress and charge it to her account. I remember one in particular, a dull grey with white trim, I brought home. From the look on Mom's face, I knew I had fallen short in the wardrobe department.

I was a tomboy, an outdoors girl, not a daughter she could dress up and show off to her friends. So she handed me over to my father, who loved having an athletic, boyish daughter whom he could teach to hunt, ride, and fish, and be comfortable in all places wild.

While I was physically more aligned with Dad, Mom was the parent my soul gravitated towards. Although she exuded capability and organization, I was intuitively drawn to the emotional currents running deep below her surface—her loving and needy dependence on my father, her abdication of her personal power to his overwhelming will. And all I wanted to do was let her know much I loved her, how I would stand up for her and help her see how strong and wonderful she was. But in the end I failed to do even that.

My mother was intellectually "gifted", so much so that Dr. Lewis Terman of Stanford University chose her to be part of his study on people with genius IQ's. Qualifying for his ground-breaking Genetic Study of Genius, my mother was one of Dr. Terman's 1,528 youngsters (856 boys, 672 girls); they were nick-named "Termites." She never talked of this—only after she died did her best friend tell me of her intellectual excellence.

I remember her love of reading—her bedside table was covered in books—and her ability to shine in most any literary or philosophical discussion (of which there were many at our dinners). While Dad was more street smart, Mom, with her keen knowledge of music and books, was more intellectually versatile. Oddly, the subject of politics never came up, thus encouraging my lack of interest in that area.

I also remember her wonderfully optimistic sayings. Whenever she received a letter from Rusty or Hilary, who were away at boarding school, she'd exclaim, "Joy Bells! Today's a red-letter day!" If I told her of any success, however small: "Oh sweetheart, I'm over the moon!" If it were a particularly beautiful day: "It's a bluebird day, today!" If she felt unusually lucky: "I'm sitting in the catbird seat." In talking about someone wonderful (usually my father): "He hung the moon." Reassuring me I was in Dad's good graces: "You are the apple of his eye." She'd often end her letters to loved ones, "I'll be waiting for you until the cows come home," or "I'll be there to meet you with bells on!"

On the other hand, Dad never hesitated to throw out at whim as many negative sayings as he could: So-and-so is a pill (a tiresome, dull, weak, useless person) or a load of hay (usually used in a social context as someone who was so boring he/she brought down the mood of an entire dinner party) or nothing to write home about (anyone he perceived who lacked any visible merit). "Linda, stop being such a load of hay," he'd say at dinner. "Sit up straight, push those bosoms out, and say something of interest."

Dad loved commenting on women's breasts. In his opinion Mom's were perfect, but some of her friends came up lacking. Droopers and stringers were two of his favorite names. After they'd gone to an opera dinner party, he'd say, "Pat, did you happen to notice? Grace sure is getting droopers, isn't she?"

"Oh Prentis," my mother would sigh, "If you can't say something nice, please don't say anything." He laughed. "Don't be such a pill."

When May 1st arrived, Dad, after a few drinks at dinner, would start singing, "Hooray, hooray, the first of May, outdoor screwing starts today." Mom would whisper, "Prentis, please not in front of the children." Then she would press the button under her chair to summon Adrian and Gee, who would rush in, Gee placing a shrimp cocktail in front of each one of us, Adrian pouring Stony Hill chardonnay into our wine glasses, including Hap's, who was nine at the time.

An only child of absent divorced parents, Mom had little

family other than the one she and Dad created. And that was where she found her emotional support. In the opinion of her family and friends, Mom truly loved Dad with all her heart. Over and over she would say, "Your father and I were meant to be. We are soul mates." Dad talked constantly of his love for her and often mentioned, in front of company, how great she was in bed. Often at dinner he would reach over and grab her breast, something that made me cringe.

He set such a high bar that I worried I'd never be able to find that one perfect mate and create such a successful marriage as theirs. I never heard them argue (Dad once told me they only disagreed over the handling of us four children), and I never realized Dad was womanizing throughout most of their marriage until a few years before Mom died.

In the final part of her life, Dad said some very cruel words to her and flaunted his affair with Denise, but she still couldn't admit to herself that he no longer loved her. To destabilize her further, to make it seem as if she, not he, was the problem, he arranged for her to see a psychiatrist. Finally, with the doctor's help she understood that Dad—the very person who had insisted we always tell the truth ("An omission is as bad as a commission") or face serious consequences—had been lying to her and lying for much of their marriage.

Devastated, she confided in her best friend that her unfailing belief in her husband was shattered. Throughout their 33-year marriage, he had her convinced he'd never lied to her. "The one thing I knew I could always count on was Prentis being truthful to me," she told her friend. "Now I no longer can."

Two weeks before Mom died, I went over to 2920 Broadway,

my family home until I married. I found her in the living room visiting with one of her many friends. After we hugged, I sat down to chat. Asking us to wait a minute, Mom went upstairs, then returned with all the jewelry Dad had given her over the years. She spread it out on the couch, touching each piece, reminiscing about the occasion of each gift. She had even saved his love notes that accompanied them.

At the time I thought it was odd; uncomfortable with this uncharacteristic behavior and not wanting to acknowledge her despair, I left soon thereafter. I never saw my mother alive again. When she died so suddenly, I mourned not only her death but also the incompleteness of our relationship. I often wondered if I could have said or done something that day that would have lifted her broken heart and perhaps prevented her death.

In retrospect I admitted the obvious: She had been trying to convince herself—with her close friend and daughter as witnesses—that Dad did once cherish and love her. Ashamed, I blamed myself for not being more of an emotional support for her in this terrible time of need. Unable to imagine her final seconds, I was also devastated that so gentle a woman could die so violently. With my mother gone, although my father never knew it, he lost the lifeline to his heart. So did our family. Filled with unresolved feelings and questions, her death started me on my journey to understand who I was, and how I wanted to live what had been up to then a superficial, unexamined life.

WHAT DOES IT MEAN TO BE BRAVE?

Dad put a great premium on physical bravery. At four, I already knew if I climbed to the top rung of the corral fence, if I gathered eggs from the tough Bantam hens without flinching, if I didn't cry when I fell, or if I could ride without a lead, I would earn Dad's favor. I still look at the photo of Dad on Diablo, and me, a tiny bump on top of old Barney's back, riding across the wide gravel bar of Sulphur Creek.

At eight, I was practicing hitting tin cans with our .22 rifle, in anticipation of shooting my first buck when I reached 10. By 11, my parents gave me free rein on our 10,000-acre ranch, as long as I told someone my plans and my expected time of return. Lizzie, my best friend, and I would ride our horses for hours, crossing Fraser Creek, where we could see the Geysers spouting in the distance, and heading into the cooler terrain of springs and watercress.

In San Francisco I either walked to my destinations (school, St. Mary the Virgin church, California Tennis Club) or took the 3 Jackson or 22 Fillmore buses. I never remember worrying about finding my way, nor did I feel anxious about being on my own. When I was just 13, my mother took me to boarding school in Connecticut, helped me unpack, gave me a huge hug and left. After that one cross-country flight together, I was on my own. Fortunately, I had a glorious time talking through the night and playing cards.

At 17, I went to college in upstate New York. I can still picture myself, in heels and gloves, and lugging a heavy suitcase, scanning the board for the train to Poughkeepsie. Again, I had no trouble finding my way. Fortunate to have parents during these early years who loved to travel and include their four children in some of their adventures, I was exposed to incredible places: Mozambique, Kenya, Switzerland, France, Italy, Alaska, to name a few. I was excited and eager to see the world.

My persona was that of a brave, outdoorsy young woman who pushed her physical limits and felt comfortable finding her way. And I knew in doing so, I was earning Dad's approval. In Switzerland, when I was 13, our ski instructor asked who wanted to climb (with skins on our skis) above where the lifts ended and then ski down in untouched snow. I and two others volunteered. During our ascent I remember questioning whether I would make it (in French I kept repeating to myself, "It's necessary I keep going.") I did, and after finally reaching the summit, our thrilling ski down was well worth our efforts. When I recounted my experience to my family, Dad's eyes shone, while my siblings were unimpressed.

In 1965 Hap, my younger brother, and I accompanied Mom and Dad to Kenya to shoot elephants. By this time, I had my doubts. I didn't want to shoot any more animals, but somewhere inside I was still the father-pleasing little girl who needed to perform. Stifling my concerns, I jumped on board and began preparing for this challenge. Not strong enough to manage a .457 rifle, the appropriate one for elephant, I spent hours practicing with the 30.06 Dad gave me.

With this smaller rifle, I had to hit the elephant either in his ear hole, or—if he were charging me—in his mouth. Anywhere else the bullets wouldn't penetrate his thick hide enough to kill him. We spent days following and tracking elephants, coming within hundreds of yards of large herds grazing through the trees. As we moved closer, invariably the wind would shift, warning the elephants of our presence, and they would fade into the bush, grey shadows swallowed up by the thick brush.

One windless, hot afternoon we came across a large bull about 150 yards off, standing under the shade of a thorn tree. "You're up first, Linda," my father whispered. Terrified I would miss (and earn my father's disapproval), I could hardly hold my rifle. My hands were shaking. What if I wounded him and he charged? My brain shut down, and my body shifted into neutral. Holding my breath, I sighted in on his ear hole and squeezed the trigger. Through my scope I watched this majestic animal slide slowly down on his back haunches. Only when I exhaled did I realize he was dead.

Squaring my shoulders, I caught my father's eye. "I'm proud of you, Linda. Not many people can bring down an elephant with a 30.06—and only one shot. Well done!" In his mind, I was a "winner." Basking in the light of his approval, I felt reassured. But at that moment I vowed to myself that I would never raise a rifle to my shoulder again.

However, much to my despair, a year later my father insisted I accompany him on a Kodiak bear hunting expedition in Alaska. Still not courageous enough to risk his disapproval, and not wanting to fall off the pedestal he'd put me on, with a heavy heart, I agreed to go. We flew from Anchorage out to the Alaska Peninsula where we would spend a week in a rustic camp with two male bush pilots. On the first day there, an unexpected storm blew in. There I was, Dad's hunting companion, huddled inside a small one-room hut with three men. Waiting hours until the storm passed, I wished I were anywhere but in this wilderness.

Finally, the storm abated, and we took off in our respective planes, my father and a pilot in one, and I and the second pilot in the other. Heading in different directions, we quickly lost sight of one another. I held my breath as the plane lifted up and threaded its way through a high, narrow mountain pass and then dipped low down over the stark tundra. All I saw was endless white punctuated by black rock outcroppings. Looking for bear, we skimmed along the gray water and then circled over a low ridge.

Clouds started building up, obscuring my view out the tiny window. The pilot talked quickly into his radio; there was no response. Tossed about by sudden winds, our plane shuddered. We climbed almost to the top of the same pass and then turned back down again, repeating this maneuver for almost an hour before the pilot was finally able to make it over. During this entire time, oblivious to the danger we were in, I was relaxed and unafraid. Only when I heard the pilot exclaim, "Thank God!" did I realize we had been in terrible trouble. But I was still Dad's fearless partner who tried never to admit any weakness.

From that point on, we always kept each other in sight. On the last day, we spotted a bear lumbering down a rocky ridge. Landing on a tiny, pebbled beach, we checked the direction of the wind and began to stalk our prey. Knowing this was our last and only chance to kill a bear, I assumed I wouldn't have to perform. But as we got closer to our prey, Dad turned to me. "Linda, I've thought long and hard about this, and I want you to have this chance of a lifetime." I argued in vain.

If I refused, I was a coward; if I missed, I was a failure. At 20 I didn't understand that it was O.K. to fail. I only knew that Dad loved me when I was a courageous winner and didn't when I was not. Reluctantly, I followed my guide. As I readied myself, the wind shifted, warning the bear of our presence and driving him away from us directly towards my father. We heard a single shot, and then saw my father at the crest of the ridge, signaling thumbs up.

Profoundly relieved I was spared, I feel an angel must have been there by my side. After this trip, I ended my rifle-hunting days, outgrowing the need to be Dad's Annie Oakley. In looking back, I wonder how I was able to be so mentally and physically fearless.

Before I had children, I had few physical fears, and absolutely no fear connected to skiing. At Sugar Bowl I loved hopping on a chairlift alone, especially enjoying the beautiful vistas and the steep cliffs below, the higher I went. After the birth of my three sons, slowly I changed. Eventually I never rode the chair alone, and if it stopped unexpectedly, I felt like jumping, no matter how high we were off the ground. I was still an outdoors girl, a gamer, but I was feeling less adventuresome.

Fortunately, Bill, my strong, no-worries husband, was more than willing to calm my fears. We traveled abroad and also spent many wonderful times in outdoor pursuits—camping and fishing in Montana, bird hunting in Spain and Mexico, duck hunting in Northern California, fly fishing in Argentina. With Bill by my side, I felt safe. And though I was more timid physically, I began to take greater risks emotionally. In therapy I faced what was happening to our family, painful as that was, and began the long journey home to myself. I wrote my memoir, *Beyond His Control*, and will always wonder whether I could have been brave enough to do so without Bill's incredible support.

After he died, however, I felt my fears tumbling through me, almost paralyzing me. In the middle of the night I would wake up, disoriented and afraid of how I would keep going. Never the best navigator, I now had trouble finding my way outside of Marin, choosing to stay as close to home as possible. The idea of flying to LA and back was daunting, as was any road trip that crossed a bridge.

During this time, I finished *The Love of Angels*, a book of stories about the role of angels in our lives. As timid as I had become in forcing myself out in the physical world, I was opening up more and more to my emotional one, realizing it also takes real courage to be vulnerable and heart connected.

One black, starry night at the ranch so many years ago, my

father and I were outside on the porch. Pointing out the Big Dipper, he said, "Linda, follow the two bottom stars to the very bright one—the North Star. If you know where that is, you will never get lost." I trusted him then, but as I grew older, somehow I stopped believing I could find my way.

TWO MOTHERS

W hen my mother was pregnant with me, she never had
to wear maternity clothes. Aside from her close friends
and family, few were aware of her condition, until I decided to
arrive two months early. Weighing four pounds, one ounce, I
spent the first month of my life in an incubator before I was
brought home to the arms of Frances, my beloved nurse.

Spending most of my time with her for the first six years of
my life, I felt happy and secure. She was the one who tucked me
in at night, read to me, wiped my brow when I was feverish,
hugged me when I skinned my knee, tied colorful ribbons in my
hair. She taught me to read when I was four. With Frances always
by my side, I laughed and danced and kicked my chubby legs
hard to run into her open arms.

A tomboy, in faded blue jeans and a plaid snap button
cowboy shirt, I loved riding horseback, running, jumping, climb-
ing. Of course, many times I'd fall, my arms and legs taking a

daily beating. Years later Frances wrote me of some of her memories at the ranch. "Linda, do you remember when you were little how you practically never cried if you fell? Before you'd hit the ground, you would start saying, *It didn't hurt, it didn't hurt.*"

I turned to her for everything, while my mother drifted on the periphery—a sweet scent of perfume, a rustle of a silk party dress, the tip-tap of high heels on our polished wood floors, a soft hand brushing my cheek. When I was just six, Frances left abruptly with no goodbyes; I was inconsolable. I felt as if my world no longer had any bearings, any safe places.

When I asked my mother when Frances would return, she responded with a wave of her hand. "Linda, she's on vacation. We're not sure when she'll be back." And then a stern Miss Cooke, whose main job was caring for Hap, my new baby brother, arrived. My heart sank. No one ever told me Frances was never returning, and for many months I held onto the hope she would. Alone in my room, I compulsively kept watch, looking out my window, balancing on one foot and then the other, willing her to appear on the sidewalk below.

To my anguished questions, my parents answered vaguely, then said to stop asking—and please stop the tears as well. Frantic that my mother might leave me as Frances had, I complied. I turned to my mother and hung on to her for dear life. I wrote her notes, telling her how much I loved her. I would leave them everywhere, on her pillow where she would find them when she came home late from a party, in her dressing room drawers, even in the toes of her black satin evening shoes.

At six, I was deemed old enough to join the family for dinner. I was outgoing and full of energetic opinions, sure that Frances was going to return and have my back. One night I said something—I don't remember what—and everyone was silent. Then Dad said loudly, "Linda, where were you when the brains were passed out?" When I started to cry, he sent me to my room.

Over time, I realized I could no longer be the Linda I was with Frances. In order to hang onto my place in the family, I stopped expressing my own opinions for fear of incurring Dad's wrath. And I worried my mother might leave me as Frances had if I were too troublesome, so I tried to hide this sad/bad little girl to the best of my ability.

I remember an incident of Dad's meanness soon after I was sent away from the table. I was feeling lonely, worrying about whether Frances would ever return. We were at the ranch. Dad took me on a hike, the very same one that had been a favorite of Frances' and mine.

Since our last time there, the foreman had grazed his cattle in those fields, so I had my first glimpse of cow pies. I found I could use them as stepping stones, and I made up a game of jumping from one to the next without touching the dry grass beneath. What I didn't know, and my father did, was that they all weren't dried out. Some were fresher than others. He later told me he was waiting for me to land on one that was soft.

Eventually, of course, I did. I slipped and got cow manure all over me—on my jeans, my hands, even in my face and hair —then burst into tears. My father laughed and once again said, "How can anyone be so stupid?" Suddenly I felt Frances nearby and even turned to see if she had by some miracle returned. No one was by my side, but I remember the feeling I had of her reassuring presence. I turned to Dad and said in a loud voice, "How can you be so mean to such a beautiful little girl?"

He didn't answer, and we walked back to the house in silence. I later overheard his telling my mother how spoiled I was because of Frances' influence and that it was a good thing he'd fired her.

Looking back, I realize Frances had been willing to put her job on the line to shield me from Dad's temper. She gave me the strength I needed for the future to stand up to him and his abusive power plays, something none of my siblings were able to do. Her sturdy love and my mother's as well ultimately guided me home to myself.

After my mother died when I was 23, I became an emotional explorer, on a never-ending journey to seek connection and fill that lost part of myself. I was always on the lookout for a mother. Soaking up whatever love I could find, I found bits and pieces of mothers in her friends.

Outgoing, energetic and strong, Ellie Sharp came closest to replacing her. We skied, played bridge, fished and hunted together, all activities I had shared with my mother. Kind and generous, she, too, loved entertaining all ages at her elegant dinner parties. Unlike my mother, Ellie was a survivor and never could understand how Mom put up with my father's abusive actions for so long. "I would have kicked him out, that SOB," she said once when we were sitting in the duck blind.

Recently while fishing the lower Sacramento River with John, I inhaled the pungent smell of bay trees lining the banks and was transported back to the HE Ranch of my youth. These trees lined the spring where my mother and I would stop to water our horses in the shade.

One still, hot August day she took me riding. When we reached Fraser Creek, she slid gracefully off her saddle. Holding one rein of Dune's bridle, she patted the ground next to her. I sat down quietly with Tickle's rein in my hand. Touching shoulders, we watched both horses suck in the clear water and then nibble bits of fresh watercress that lined the banks. I felt I was the luckiest girl in the world.

My mother was at her happiest when she was at the ranch with her family. Wandering through her rose garden, I would watch her clip her favorites for a centerpiece that would grace our long, dark wooden table, where later over dinner we would meet to share our adventures. Candles highlighted the fragrant beauty of the flowers.

As always, Mom was seated on Dad's right, her elegance detailed in her straight back and simple V-neck black cashmere sweater. Her eyes alight, she captured me in her glance and softly patted her heart. I share her love of flowers, especially roses, and make sure I always have them blooming throughout my small house.

Another memory, a terrible one, tugs at my heart. Just six months before Mom's death, with summer gone and Dad mostly away on 'business' trips, she invited me to accompany her to her godchild's wedding in Los Angeles. At the reception one of the guests, a psychic, was giving palm readings. For some reason she was drawn to my mother. Holding her hand, the psychic looked at her palm for several long minutes and then dropped it casually, saying she was out of practice.

Later pulling me aside, the psychic said, in a low, urgent voice, "Something devastating will happen to your mother unless she asks for help. She must let down her guard and share her feelings with someone she trusts."

Since Mom never confided in me about her unraveling marriage, I chose to play along with the party line, pretending that I, as well, knew nothing about my father's affair with Denise. Near the end of her life, only once did I see her break down. We were having dinner in our San Francisco home when she put her face in her hands and wept in front of the servants.

When that happened, I imagined myself back at the ranch, where I could smell the skunk cabbage spread out across the riverbed of Sulphur Creek; where I could lie on my back and close my eyes and hear a red-tailed hawk cry his lonely, fierce hunting call; where I could feel the wind on my face that dries my tears. I could also see my parents together, riding side by side across the gravel bar, my father on Diablo, a black stallion, my mother on Dune, a white Arabian mare. Dad leaned over to say something, and in a flash, they were off, cantering towards the river.

In life my mother didn't believe in herself enough, a pattern I copied for many years after her death. I pray she is looking down and understanding now what a splendid human being she was, how much her family and friends loved her, how her sweet, gentle soul was stronger than any worldly power Dad could wield. I wish I could have reassured her of Dad's love, but by then it was too late.

At 59 he'd chosen a new path, one pulling him irrevocably into the material world, erasing all memory of love. I wish, too, Dad had been brave enough to tear down his tough, macho façade and honor his feelings. But I believe Mom now understands what I finally do as well, that even though he chose to turn away from his heart, she was always his beloved.

For years I struggled with the painful repercussions of Dad's role in taking away the two people I loved most before I left home. Had I known that I would lose Frances when I was only six and Mom when I was 23, would I have been less cavalier about their presence in my life? Probably not. When Frances left, I was too young to understand loss until I was faced with the unbearable reality of her absence. And with Mom, I just never imagined she would die so unexpectedly.

Bill's death magnified the importance of people I have loved, those who have passed and those who are still in my life. I see more clearly how Frances with her solid strength and my mother with her kind, loving ways have sustained and guided me. Their absence has made their light shine more brightly. Bill's passing taught me the importance of not taking people I love here for granted, of letting them know what they mean to me. I check in more often, take time to call or write a note. In any way I can, I try to communicate my love to my family, my friends, to anyone who touches my life.

DARING GREATLY

In 1994, Mary Keil and I collaborated on a book about friendships between women entitled *Come Rain or Come Shine*. We interviewed many women and shared our own stories as well. In the process we both learned how healthy friendships, integral to the spiritual fabric of our lives, embody universal themes of loving kindness, trust, honesty, courage, and sensitivity.

After I read Brene Brown's incredible book *Daring Greatly*, where she explores the importance of being vulnerable, I realized Mary and I should have had a chapter on this topic. Brown paints spiritual courage as daring to present our true, imperfect selves to the world, to tell our story and own it, no matter how flawed it may be. Being vulnerable, she feels, is the cornerstone for meaningful relationships.

When we feel ashamed and unlovable, we often shut ourselves off from being vulnerable, thus missing out on experi-

encing deep connections of the heart. Instead we feel discon-
nected, lonely, outside of life. Vulnerability is about sharing our
feelings and experiences with others who are open and understanding and whom we have learned to trust. Martin Buber
wrote, "When two people relate to each other authentically, God
is the electricity that surges between them."

In *The Gifts of Imperfection*, Brene Brown shares her definition of love based on her data:

"We cultivate love when we allow our most vulnerable and
powerful selves to be deeply seen and known, and when we
honor the spiritual connection that grows from that offering with
trust, kindness, and affection.

"Love is not something we give or get; it is something that
we nurture and grow, a connection that can only be cultivated
between two people when it exists within each one of them—we
can only love others as much as we love ourselves.

"Shame, blame, disrespect, betrayal and the withholding of
affection damage the roots from which love grows. Love can
only survive these injuries if they are acknowledged, healed, and
rare."

In hiding our flaws and striving for perfection, we can
suppress our shameful feelings and make ourselves fit in but we
still yearn to belong. Yet we need to be true to ourselves. When
we are brave enough to explore our darkness, we can then mani-
fest the power of our light and speak authentically.

Until my mother died the Hale Family seemed perfect to
outsiders. And we all played a part in promoting this image.
Even though as a teenager I was beginning to see some cracks in
our façade, I didn't want to look at my father's infidelities any

more than my mother did. I still sat on Dad's pedestal—in his mind, a smart, accomplished feather in his cap. In reality, I was riddled with insecurities and worried I would never live up to his expectations. I was terrified of standing up to him and falling off his pedestal. And I had no voice of my own.

Only when my mother shot herself did I know—finally—that I could no longer pretend, that I had to begin to own my story, flawed as it was. I dug through layers of shameful feelings—I am not enough, I am not loveable, I am a loser—and claimed positive ones I had felt for the first six years of my life. With Frances by my side, I had a wonderful sense of belonging, of feeling important and beloved, that I lost after she left.

In therapy I began that heart-breaking-wide-open journey back to my true self. Not until I was 40 with Bill by my side did I challenge my father to be accountable, both emotionally and financially. I had to speak up and honor my mother who hadn't; I couldn't live with myself any longer being silent and acquiescent. Instead I began remembering the Linda I was with Frances and the Linda I was becoming with Bill's support.

I knew Dad would have great difficulties forgiving me, but I never dreamt he would forever oust me from my family of origin, that up to then I had clung on to as my anchor, my place of belonging. In *Braving the Wilderness,* Brene Brown writes of true belonging as standing alone and braving the wilderness of vulnerability and criticism.

Her definition of the quest for true belonging is as follows: "True belonging is the spiritual practice of believing in and belonging to yourself so deeply that you can share your most authentic self with the world and find sacredness in both being a part of something and standing alone in the wilderness. True belonging doesn't require you to change who you are; it requires you to be who you are."

As a widow, I see more clearly how Bill's belief in me helped me to take that big step into the wilderness. Many times he would say, "Linda, you are stronger than you think; you can do whatever you put your mind and heart to." Now four years after his passing, I am left with memories that stream through me, casting light along my path. Bill continues to remind me that I must make time to discover my star and acknowledge the importance of becoming authentic, a gift God offers all of us to experience in this life. I am filled with gratitude for Bill's encouragement from beyond to be strong, to forgive, and continue to love, even those who will disown it totally.

MY MOTHER, MY ANGEL

Forty years after Mom died, I still couldn't accept the unresolved circumstances of her death. Did she take her own life or did my father shoot her, as many people thought? Either scenario was devastating, as was the not knowing. While Bill and I were still living in San Francisco, I had a reading with an Intuitive who knew only my first name and phone number. Finally I received a definitive but painful, answer.

A few minutes into the reading, she stopped abruptly and said, "Is there anyone in your family whose name starts with "M"? I think and think. "No," I said, "No name comes to my mind." She pressed me. "Are you certain?" Anyone whose name begins with M-A-R, perhaps a Marie?" Suddenly I knew. "Mari-alice," I said. "It's the formal name of my mother who died in 1969. But everyone called her Pat."

"Yes," the Intuitive said, "Your mother is here. She wants you to know she's very proud of you and the way you've raised your boys. She's telling me she wasn't strong enough. She was at her wits' end and thought she was worthless. Even though she had children, she felt she had no other way out. She didn't want people fussing over her. She is showing me her body lying in a corner. She did this herself. But it's all healed and forgiven now between your parents. And she's forgiven herself, too. Now she is a healing soul on the other side."

Overwhelmed by her accuracy I couldn't stop crying. The Intuitive continued, "Your mother wants you to be strong because she was not. She tells me she visits you in a room on the second floor of your home, on the right side of the house as you face it from the street. That's where she feels the most comfortable. That's where she brings you light. She wants to give you a big hug and tell you how proud she is of your books. She feels she's helped you in your writing. She's handing me something she wants to give to you, a rose."

Everything the Intuitive told me rang true. At the end of her life, Mom had lost her emotional strength, devastated by my father's mean words and actions. Supposedly she'd shot herself with my father's pistol, but there were inconsistent, puzzling details surrounding her death that made me and others wonder. Now I knew the answer.

What feels accurate to me as well is my mother visiting me in my study and feeling most comfortable there. After all, for years before it became my workplace, it was the nursery, occupied first by Christian, then John and finally Nick. Several times I would sense her presence as I sat reading to them at night. My mother loved books, but more than that, she would have doted on her grandchildren. I also know I could never have written *Beyond*

His Control, a memoir about my difficult relationship with my father, without sensing her support.

When the healer tells me my mother wants to give me a big hug, I cry even more, because in life, while she was kind and loving, she was preoccupied as well. Many times when she would stroke my hair or touch my arm, I wished instead she would hug me strongly, holding me for minutes close to her heart. When the healer says my mother is offering me a rose, our favorite flower, I know for certain she is an angel watching over me.

The Intuitive continues, "Your mother is mentioning a bathtub." As the wife of a demanding executive, mother of four children, and active in the San Francisco community, my mother was busy. At six I figured out the best way to have her all to myself was to sit by her side as she was taking her nightly bath. Comforted by her nearness and the fragrant smell of her lemon soap, I would dip my hands into the warm water and slide my chubby fingers over her shoulders and arms. She would turn towards me and smile.

Emotionally elusive in life, despairing as she neared death, my beloved mother now surrounds me with her strength and absolute love. I realize she has always been nearby guiding me, and I feel certain she will continue to follow me through this life's journey.

THE CIRCLE OF LOVE

PART III

THE GREAT ALONE

My daughter-in-law, Kris, gave me *The Great Alone*, a wonderful novel by Kristin Hannah. The author explores big themes: love and loss, abuse of power, dysfunctional family relationships, and forgiveness. Telling the heartbreaking story of a family—mother, father, and Leni, their 13 year-old-daughter—she writes of their moving to Alaska to start their lives afresh and of the tremendous challenges, both emotional and physical, they undergo.

Leni and her mother were extremely close. Near the end of the book, her mother died when Leni was in her early 20's. She was devastated. I could instantly relate to her grief because I was 23 when my mother unexpectedly passed and also understood why Kris was so drawn to this story. Growing up, she struggled with wanting more love and attention from her mother, who was otherwise preoccupied with her own life issues.

Happily married to my oldest son for 20 years, Kris is a

sparkling delight, a wonderful wife and devoted mother to Katie and Sam, a dear friend, capable teacher, and ceramicist. Raised by a hands-off, emotionally elusive mother, Kris was used to going it alone. Early on in our relationship, she made it clear to me I wasn't to give advice or try to act as her mother in any way. While at times I've wanted to put in my two bits' worth, to edge closer to her, I've held back, respecting her boundaries.

Kris is now struggling with her mother's dementia. She feels as if she is losing her mother before she found her. She wonders if on her next visit, her mother will even recognize her. Trying to find words to ease her pain, I say I understand her journey, her search for a mother whom she felt she lost years ago.

There is a long pause in our conversation, and then Kris says what for years I have been longing to hear, "Well, I have you." I think my heart will burst. "Yes," I answer, my throat constricting. "Yes, you do. I will never leave you."

IT'S NOT THE END OF THE TRAIL

During our many summers in Montana, Bill and I were graced with some wonderful friendships. For starters, Norma and Charlie Hughes come to mind. Third generation Montanans, they met in Ovando, where they married and worked as partners on their ranch for 57 years before Charlie passed on. He was the love of her life and vice versa.

Today I called Norma, to wish her a happy birthday. She is 89! Bursting with positive, loving energy, she is still very active in running their ranch. "If we can dry out, we'll have a good hay crop this summer. And I've planted carrots, beets, cabbage, onion, spuds, and lettuce in my garden.

"And the flowers—oh, how I love flowers! I have petunia, pansy, delphinium, larkspur, snap dragon, and you should see the iris. They come in so many colors—white tops with gold, apricot, lavender, pink, yellow." I ask her about the cows. "I worry when I put them out in the pasture; so far I haven't had a sighting of a wolf. But I have my rifle ready in case. And I just saw a mama grizzly today with three cubs. Can you imagine that?"

Without a pause, she continues, "Oh, I miss my Charlie more now, but he still helps me all the time. I'll not know what to decide and then I do, and it's Charlie who's directing me. I think of him every day. I know when it's my turn on the roll call, he will be there waiting for me."

"Do you really believe this?" I ask.

"Yes, yes, I do."

"So do I," I say, comforted by her understanding and faith.

Her courage, generous heart, and reverence for nature are parts of the fabric of her gossamer being that light up the lives of all who know and love her. Days later she sends me the following poem that was read at Charlie's memorial.

It's not the end of the trail for me;
I've just traveled on, you see,
Up ahead where greener pastures grow
And cool water streams dance as they flow.
Flowers in bloom of every sort and kind,
Colors more vivid than any I left behind,
Family and friends I haven't seen in years,
Hugs and handshakes and no more tears.
They've welcomed me home here today,
A place of peace for me to stay.
They say it's my home for eternity;
No, it's not the end of the trail for me.

I feel certain that Charlie and Bill are together, keeping watch and waiting for Norma and me to walk that trail home to them.

LOVE IN A BOOKMARK

The other day I opened a letter from Laura, my much younger friend who lives 2,000 miles away. We rarely see each other, but there is a strong thread of love that connects us. We first met when she was three and I was 25. It was before I'd had children, and I was much more interested in flirting with her father than paying attention to this adorable child.

Undeterred, she made a beeline for my lap, where she sat entranced with my purse. She loved rummaging through it. At times hopping off, she'd walk around holding my purse and laugh, and then she'd run back to sit with me. My future husband and her father became friends, and I'd see Laura occasionally. She grew up to be a wonderful, lovely young woman; she married and now has a daughter of her own.

Recently, she called to ask about my new book, *The Love of Angels,* which I immediately sent to her. She wrote in return:

"I was so excited to receive your book. I have always

believed in angels and enjoy reading about others' encounters with them. I started it immediately, but as the mother of a teenage girl, I am interrupted on a fairly regular basis. I thought, Oh my, I need to mark the page, but I didn't want to harm the book in any way.

"Out of the blue I remembered the bookmark my father had given me when I was a teenager. It was a monogrammed sterling silver one. I loved slipping it into whatever book I was reading, so I could easily find my place where I had stopped. Over the years with the development of computers and e-books, I didn't use this lovely gift as much as I had, and eventually put it in the back of a drawer and forgot about it.

"After a long search, I found it. It was tarnished, but I cleaned it with silver polish and it sparkled! With a big smile on my face, I marked the page in your book. Right then I had a strong feeling that Dad and Bill were watching over you and me and delighting in the fact we have this great friendship. What a wonderful way to begin 2018!"

ANGELS OF LIGHT

Since angels are beings of pure energy, they can appear as a friend, or a flower or bird, in a dream or a song. They inspire us to love. Recently I heard a story about a fellow member of our tennis club that I wished I could have shared with Bill. It was a very hot day, and this man was hitting against the ball machine. On the court next to him, two women (who normally never use the court adjacent to the practice one) were playing. Suddenly, they saw the man drop to the ground.

Rushing over, they knelt on either side. One woman just happened to have her cell phone handy, and the other one happened to be a nurse and she administered CPR immediately. From what I learned, he remembers hovering above his body and seeing family and friends who had already passed over. He wanted to join them. But then he heard a loud voice. "It's not your time. Look down and you will see two angels with you."

Doing as he was told, he saw two pools of golden light, one on either side of him, and it was then that he returned to his earthly body. He is convinced that four angels saved his life that day.

BILLY GRAHAM

I read Peggy Noonan's fine article, "Billy Graham, The Ecumenical Evangelist," in *The Wall Street Journal*, just days after his death. She paints a wonderful picture of him, a man who preached to huge groups of people, touching millions of lives, but who also had the ability to reach into the individual soul and convince that person God was interested in him personally.

Graham promoted a worldwide view of Christian unity and cooperation. When his son asked him what he wanted on his gravestone, he said "Preacher." I love what Graham said: "Someday you will read or hear that Billy Graham is dead. Don't you believe a word of it. I shall be more alive than I am now. I will just have changed my address. I will have gone into the presence of God."

THE DITZY-PAT STAR

I had a childhood friend named Charlotte. Her mother, Ditzy, was my mother's best friend, and so growing up, our lives were intertwined. When my mother died, I turned to Ditzy, who simply stepped in where Mom had been and helped to fill that empty place.

When Charlotte was teaching in China, Ditzy died unexpectedly. I spent some time with my friend when she returned for the funeral, and she told me she had sent in to the U.C. Berkeley Astronomy Department to have a star named after both our mothers—the Ditzy-Pat Star.

Now I can picture them whenever I look up into a black, starry sky. I see them laughing and gossiping. They are both newlyweds again, eager and in love and ready to take on the world. They put their arms around each other's waists and walk in step, high heels clicking, purses swinging, gloves in hand, and certainly some wonderful scarf around their necks. Imagining them together, perhaps perched on this star, eases my aching heart.

Charlotte wrote me after she returned to China: "It's cloudy and overcast here in Chengdu, so I mostly stargaze in my mind. Still, I inquire, 'Star light, star bright, which star do I see tonight?' and the Ditzy-Pat Star always answers. I went to my Chinese church today, and Minister Li was telling the Christmas story. He ended it with a metaphor. The story is love. The power of association is a wondrous thing, and my mind became a mass of images of the beach. I was five years old and Ditzy and Pat were both watching over me as I lay in an oxygen tent. I remembered having asthma, not being able to breathe, but I also remembered the touch of four maternal hands. Linda, we should be so proud of our mothers."

I saved this special letter and would read it from time to time. A few years later Charlotte, too, died. Now I know they are together, all three, the light of the Ditzy-Pat Star shining more brightly than ever.

BORN ON CHRISTMAS DAY

One long afternoon, I was working on my taxes with my accountant (something Bill always did when he was alive). When we took a break, I asked about his son, an impressive young man. Leaning back in his chair, my accountant said, "Do you want to hear a story?" "Yes!" I said, happy to be distracted from the financial situation at hand.

"My wife and I always wanted to have children," he explained, "but after 15 years of marriage with no babies in sight, we decided to adopt. Choosing the private adoption route, we soon found a willing couple. In return for our paying all medical expenses during the pregnancy and delivery, they agreed to give us the baby at birth in the hospital. We signed a voluntary contract and then eagerly waited.

"In early December they called to say labor had begun. We immediately flew to Las Vegas and arrived at the hospital just as our baby was being born. The nurses told us she was a healthy girl, and we were overwhelmed with joy. When we joined the couple in their hospital room later that day, we sensed something was wrong.

"Just when we thought we were becoming new parents, they announced they'd decided to keep the baby. (Later, we found out it was a scam; they'd never intended on giving up their child; they'd just needed money to pay their expenses.) Stunned, we stumbled out the door. Even though the nurses tried their best to console us, my wife grew hysterical. "During the long trip home, she couldn't stop weeping no matter what I said or did. Helpless, I sat silently in our grief.

"We had little enthusiasm for celebrating Christmas. My wife folded up the baby clothes and blankets, and I dismantled the crib. With heavy hearts, we bought and decorated a Christmas tree, but nothing could alleviate our disappointment.

"On December 24 the phone rang. My wife answered. It was one of the nurses from the hospital telling her that a young woman in labor had just come in. She had told them she couldn't afford to keep her baby and asked us if we knew of a good, loving family who might want a baby at such short notice. 'All of us here at the hospital immediately thought of you,' the nurse added. 'Can you get here soon?'

"We caught the next flight to Las Vegas and were there in the hospital when the young woman gave birth to a beautiful, perfect boy on Christmas Day. The adoption papers were signed, and we went to meet our baby son. Holding him for one last time, the birth mother said how grateful she was to know her baby would grow up with loving, supportive parents. She then motioned us to her side. Her eyes shining, my wife reached out her arms and picked up our son with the greatest of care, holding him gently next to her heart. We flew home with the most precious gift we've ever received.

"A few days later I was driving on the freeway. I turned on the radio to a station I usually never listen to. I heard the voice of an evangelist say, 'The theme of my homily today is God's delays are not God's denials.' I felt as if he were speaking directly to me; no truer words had I heard. My heart was full. I wish I'd been able to tell Bill this great story!"

SOPHIA AND YAYA

Sophia, my six-year-old granddaughter, believes in fairies, and at 75, I still do as well. When I was her age, I saw them everywhere, mostly outdoors, perched on a daisy, darting through the shiny green camellia leaves of our San Francisco garden, or just hovering above where our taciturn snapping turtle lay, the sunlight catching the sparkle of their tiny wings. They were there, and then they were gone.

Always on the lookout, I reported every sighting to Frances, my nurse. "Ah!" she'd laugh. "What color were the wings this time?" "Pink," I'd say, standing next to my mother's favorite rose bush. When I went to bed at night, I'd say my prayers with Frances, remembering to thank God and the fairies for loving us.

One afternoon as I was wandering through the garden looking for fairies, my father put down his newspaper and said, "Linda, what are you looking for?" "Fairies," I said. "What nonsense!" he muttered, rattling his paper. "Honestly! They aren't real. You are making them up." Before I could protest, I heard Frances call me; running into her open arms, I saw a flicker of gold over her shoulder. "Yellow!" I shouted, to make sure my father heard.

The first time Sophia came to my house for lunch and an afternoon nap, her mother warned me I'd have trouble putting her down to sleep, and she was correct! I had little success. After reading Sophia a book, I gave her a kiss and left. She called out, "Yaya, come back." I relented and read her one more book. "Time for your nap," I said sternly, and then quietly left. For a long time afterwards, I heard her talking and singing, but I just let her be. When her mother picked her up, she was cranky.

The next time she came, I had an inspiration. After our book, I started telling her about fairies and how they fly around and sprinkle us with different colored fairy dust to help us go to sleep. Immediately intrigued, she asked what color were their wings? I said, "All colors. Blue, pink, lavender, gold, red, silver, and they have sparkles on them."

I told her to lie down, and then I said, "Here comes the blue (Sophia's favorite color) fairy. She's wearing a pale blue dress with bright blue sparkles on it, and her wings are blue, too. And she has blue fairy dust in her hand. As I danced my fingers lightly on Sophia's shoulder and across her back, I said, "Oh, she's a dancing fairy!" As I ran my fingers through Sophia's hair, I said, "Oh, she's sprinkling her special fairy dust now."

Sophia was asleep in no time. Every subsequent nap we came up with different colored fairies, and soon Sophia was telling me which ones were coming and what they were wearing. Naps under her mother's watch became problematic, because Marcela, a terrific parent, had no idea what her daughter was talking about! But soon she understood and played our game with great success.

At Sophia's fourth birthday party, Marcela bought fairy wings as favors for all the girls to wear. They were an instant hit. I watched from across the park as seven little girls, wearing wings of lavender, blue, pink, yellow, and green, were running full speed with their arms outstretched, laughing, spinning, dancing. In and out of a grove of redwood trees they raced, sunlight bouncing off their wings in rainbow colors of light. Sophia, her pale blue wings sparkling, led the way. Once again, I was four and filled with wonder and delight.

AN UNEXPECTED GIFT

Twenty-eight years ago, I was raising money for Grace Cathedral to fund the new library in memory of my mother. One day I opened a letter from a Radine Hoag with a check enclosed for the library. I had never heard of this person. Curious and grateful, I called John Bryan, my closest cousin at that time, who knew much about our family history, and he explained who this mysterious donor was.

Radine's Aunt Linda was my grandmother. I was intrigued; I have few relatives. My mother was an only child of divorced parents, and my father, the only child of Prentis and Linda Hale. Both my grandfathers died before I was born, and I never recall my parents mentioning either one. I can count on one hand the times I saw my two grandmothers.

I can only conclude that my mother was not close to her mother, for reasons I will never know, because she never talked of her or invited her to visit. I did hear from whispered comments that my father and his mother (Radine's aunt) had a bitter falling-out and didn't speak for many years. In both cases, neither ever came to our house for family events.

Listening to my friends' descriptions of large, boisterous holiday celebrations, I was caught up in their excitement and yearned for more family to materialize. But only immediate family gathered for our Christmases, birthdays, and other holidays, a small island unto ourselves. After my mother died and our lives unraveled, I was always on the lookout for sympathetic family replacements.

Excited about this unknown relative, I called Radine and soon thereafter flew to Pasadena where we met at Huntington Gardens. Dressed in an elegant suit, her hair beautifully coiffed, she carried herself with grace and dignity. Independent and smart, she was a woman of many talents and opinions. We sat and talked for hours, and I couldn't believe my great fortune in discovering this very special relative.

Radine was very involved in the arts, volunteering her services at the Los Angeles County Museum. She talked of her deep love of family and tradition. She told me of her membership in the Mayflower Society, of which she was very proud. I found out she was the 11th generation descendant from Richard Warren, a passenger on the Mayflower voyage that terminated at Plymouth, New England, in December 1620. She was also a member of The Society of California Pioneers.

I shared her love of family and lineage, and in Radine I found a relative who was a mother surrogate, someone I had searched for since my mother died. We only met a handful of times but always kept in touch by phone and letters. Taking a great interest in my life, she was always loving and supportive. Without fail, she would ask about my husband and my three wonderful sons, then would end every conversation with "I'm so proud of you. Your Grandmother Linda also would have been happy to see how you are representing our family." Radine believed in me when no one in my immediate family did, and her love sustained me through many difficult years.

A graduate of UCLA, she was 75 when we met and had recently retired from her lifelong job at Lockheed Martin in Human Resources. I invited her several times to come visit us in San Francisco, but no matter how hard I tried to convince her, she always declined. So I settled for many phone conversations and several Los Angeles visits, and felt grateful for her emotional support.

Three years ago, when John was in the Beverly Hills Art Show, we visited Radine in her tiny rented apartment. Refusing help, at age 100, she still lived alone. Pulling a small cart, she would walk eight blocks each way to the nearest grocery store. She did her own laundry, cooked her own meals, and paid attention to every penny. She lived quietly and modestly.

Upset because she'd gone through a red light she hadn't noticed and gotten a ticket, she worried she might lose her license; subsequently she did, and with that loss of independence, she started downhill. At our last visit, she told me about an antique Japanese shawl my grandmother had given her that she wanted me to have. But she couldn't find it, and I gave it little thought. As we parted, John gave her one of his beautiful sunset ocean prints, which she loved. We hugged, and I had a feeling I wouldn't see her again as the Radine I knew.

As her living situation deteriorated, she still adamantly refused help. Finally, Melissa, her beloved cousin, called a lawyer friend, and he helped us get a conservatorship for Radine. Very much against her will, she was taken to a nursing home, where under the right medications, she calmed down and was happy and comfortable with her new situation. She joyfully celebrated her 103rd birthday there!

Two months later she had medical complications, and we were told she was weakening. John and I flew down for a final visit. In a wheelchair, she had a hard time speaking. I opened a box of See's candy, and she looked and looked at it. I pointed to my favorite, and slowly she raised her hand, lifted that piece out of the box, and took a small bite—and then another and another. She smiled.

Smoothing her soft, wispy hair away from her forehead and holding her thin, mottled hand, I put my head next to hers and said, "I love you, Radine." And I heard her whisper back, "I love you, too." Two weeks later—at 103—she died.

My mother always taught me to look for angels in the people we meet, to look beyond their exteriors, beyond whether they have power or money, into their hearts. "You never know," she'd say, "what gifts they have, what messages we need to hear."

Radine stands out in my life as one of the most special people I have ever met. When I was floundering, she reached out and steadied me; when I most needed family, she stepped in, never expecting anything in return. With her message of love, for me she was an angel.

When Radine passed, I was shocked to find out that through her hard work and frugal lifestyle, she left some money in equal parts to her beloved cousin Melissa and to me. Openhearted in life and now in death, she set an example that I will try my hardest to follow. A beacon of light that shines steadily, illuminating the path of my life, she holds a forever place in my heart. I read this piece at her memorial service (author unknown):

I am standing on the seashore. A ship at my side spreads her white sails to the morning breeze and starts for the blue ocean. She is an object of beauty and strength. I stand and watch her until at length she hangs like a speck of white cloud just where the sea and sky come to mingle with each other.

Then someone at my side says, "There she is gone."
Gone where?

Gone from my sight. That is all. She is just as large in mast and hull and spar as she was when she left my side, and she is just as able to bear her load of living freight to her destined port. Her diminished size is in me, not in her. And just at the moment when someone at my side says, "There, she is gone!" there are other eyes watching her coming, and other voices ready to take up the glad shout, "Here she comes!"

COFFEE WITH KATIE

Katie, my 18-year-old granddaughter, invited me to meet her for coffee at The Depot the other day. Thrilled, I accepted immediately. When I arrived, she was browsing through the bookstore section of this cafe, her dark blond hair framing a serious expression on her sweet face. "Hi Katie," I called. Looking up, she smiled.

When Kris, my daughter-in-law, was pregnant with Katie, everyone was quick to offer an opinion on whether she was carrying a boy or a girl. As her due date loomed, there was an almost unanimous consensus she was having a boy. Kris thought so as well. Painting the nursery blue, she had soft blue blankets ready to wrap her firstborn in, and on the closet shelves, she placed tiny blue and white outfits (and an occasional pale yellow one). There was not a doll in sight.

Perhaps influenced by wishful thinking (I am, after all, the mother of three sons), I dreamt that I was holding a tiny, baby girl, and it was then I knew I would soon have a granddaughter. On our way back from visiting Nick, our youngest, at boarding school, Christian called to say Kris had gone into labor. Excited, I said, "I hope you have some girls' names lined up!" He laughed, "Mom, you know it'll be a boy." "Don't be so sure," I said.

After a long labor, much to most everyone's surprise, Kris gave birth to a beautiful 8 lb. 9 oz. baby girl, later to be named Katherine Castle McIntosh, Katie for short. From an early age, Katie seemed wise well beyond her years. Observant with intense hazel eyes, she examined her world in depth, but at two still hadn't said many words. Nonetheless, Christian felt it was time to find a 'grandmother' name for me.

"Lala," he said one afternoon, as we were sitting with Katie, who had surrounded herself with her many stuffed animals. "No way," I replied. "That makes me sound as if I'm a lightweight!" Mimi, Gran, nothing we came up with felt right, so we dropped the subject and went on to other matters. Later as I hugged Katie goodbye, smiling, she looked at me and said, "Yaya." Instantly loving the name, I said, "Yes, I'm your Yaya, I'm your Yaya." Later I found out that it means grandmother in Greek.

Katie was always sure where she wanted to go on our outings. After I met her at preschool, we would walk, hand in hand, down Fillmore Street to Pets Unlimited, where she would make a beeline past all the dogs to the large caged area for cats. About nine in all, they were in various stages of activities: some sleeping, some perched high on a post, some stretching or eating, some chasing a toy. We were allowed to sit inside with them, and Katie never tired of watching their antics.

I remember sitting there beside my wondrous granddaughter, bathed in delight, savoring these small, authentic moments that contributed to the fabric of my happiness. I have many remembrances of Katie times, strung like pearls on a necklace I wear close to my heart.

As we sit down for coffee, she tells me how her parents now leave a sign from "Management" on her door to remind her to clean up her messy room (or else!), and I laugh, remembering how messy mine was at her age—and how John's (my middle son, the artist) was as well. "It's the sign of someone creative," Katie explains, and I of course agree. We then discuss the Myers-Briggs personality types, knowing we are both introverted, intuitive, feeling types.

As INFJ's we talk about the bigger questions like, Why are we here? What's our purpose? And what is the meaning of the life? And because we have this larger perspective, we sometimes feel like outsiders looking in. Since we each yearn for authentic connection and meaningful conversation, we consider it a gift when we find other people who understand.

Time to go, and we hug. Fighting back tears, I tell Katie how proud I am of who she is and of what she's accomplished. Mourning the passing of her childhood yet celebrating her rite of passage into a young, amazing woman, I wish her Godspeed. Memories of our 18 years together in this life tumble through me.

Yes, there is something else I want to tell her. I want her to know that it is easy to miss seeing the very people who are closest to us, how we can take for granted those family members and close friends we love the most, and how important it is to take them fully into our hearts and nourish and celebrate them instead. Oh Katie, I celebrate you, I love you, I salute you on your continuing journey in this life.

HEART AND SOUL

My mother was born into a family of musicians. In 1850 her grandfather, F. Loui King, founded the King's Conservatory of Music in San Jose, California. As Dean he attracted some of the best soloists from Europe. An exceptional pianist, Mr. King held piano recitals where he and his pupils played works of the old classical and modern composers, and where he envisioned building "the greatest musical center in America, if not in the world…a center like Bayreuth."

In looking at his portrait, I saw a strong jaw and stern, piercing eyes staring back. Once my mother told me how much she had loved sitting on his lap and reaching up to stroke his full, red beard. Clearly she adored her bigger-than-life grandfather, a strong presence who encouraged her love of music.

His son and my mother's father, Frank Giorza King, was a music instructor, composer and pianist, who taught at the King's Conservatory under the shadow of his exacting father. I never heard my mother, an only child, mention her father's name, and all I found to convince me he existed was a piece of sheet music in the bottom of her piano bench, "Impromptu in F," that he wrote in 1901. When I asked a friend to play it, I was mesmerized by its complex emotional brilliance. I can only conclude that my grandfather had been far from a solid father figure for my mother.

My mother was a talented classical pianist, and I remember sitting next to her, watching her nimble fingers fly across the keyboard. Later, because of arthritis she stopped playing, but insisted that Hilary and I take piano lessons. Hilary took to her lessons like a duck to water, but I, on the other hand, had zero musical talent. My only claim to fame was playing "March of the Wee Folk" at the Burke's School Assembly when I was in kindergarten. After Frances left two years later, I totally lost interest. In a lesson one afternoon as I was struggling to play a piece, I heard what sounded like a snort. Looking to my side, I saw that Mr. Mihailof, my strict, Russian teacher, had fallen asleep. Much to my relief, my mother ended my lessons soon after.

My parents loved all kinds of music. Mom served on the board of the San Francisco Symphony, and Dad, who had taken over his mother's box at the San Francisco Opera, served on the board and as its president. Aside from classical and opera, we loved going to musicals, and I knew the words to most of the songs from *Oklahoma, South Pacific, Carousel, Pajama Game* (the first musical my parents took me to; oh how I loved it!), *The King and I*, and many others. Dad would go on binges when he found a singer he loved: For weeks on end we'd hear Harry Belafonte, then a sudden switch to Lena Horne, then Ella Fitzgerald, and on to Matt Monro, my mother's heart throb.

Much to my despair, I could hear how a favorite piece should sound yet I could never capture that when I was singing. My voice was almost a monotone. In my next life, I vowed I would be a singer and pianist. Bill, too, loved music, and fantasized about being a conductor. And two of my three sons are very musically inclined.

Christian, my oldest, took piano lessons but then moved on to playing the bass and guitar. In high school, he started two bands, wrote original music for piano and guitar, and started collecting vinyl. In college he gave weekly bass lessons, worked at Leopold Records in Berkeley, and was a D.J. at the Ace Café. By now he has collected over 2,000 records alphabetized by genre that line a wall of his study, and he knows the history and story of each one.

His daughter, Katie, now 18, is carrying on our family's musical tradition. As a shy 5th grader she had been taking voice and guitar lessons but resisted performing for others. When her public school's annual talent show came, however, Katie surprised her parents by signing up to sing "Beautiful" by Christina Aguilera, a cappella. Standing in the back row of the gymnasium, they watched the students perform, praying that Katie would not have to follow three of the most popular girls who did a tap dance with a light show that got the entire student body yelling.

Right away they heard the announcer call out, "Now we have Katie McIntosh." Tentatively, she stepped on stage, then gave a performance that brought down the house. Since that night, Katie has sung and played the guitar many times at Sweetwater and other Northern California venues (even at The Fillmore in San Francisco). A month ago I attended her final performance at Sweetwater where she was the lead singer in an all-male band.

I remember back five years to my 70th birthday when Katie surprised me with her rendition of Elton John's "Your Song." I couldn't stop my tears. Now headed East to college, she is ready to embrace new horizons and opportunities to further expand her talents. "Katie," I will say before she leaves, "Godspeed. Now you will sing your song."

John, my middle son, also inherited Mom's musical genes. Not only did he have an incredible voice from a young age, he was drawn to my grandfather's baby grand piano in our living room in San Francisco. After he started piano lessons, he quickly was able to read the notes, but he could also play complicated classical pieces by ear. His teacher, thrilled to have a potential prodigy, encouraged him as did Bill and I.

However, he stopped his lessons in his teens but never totally let go of his interest in playing. Recently we were at a friend's house, and John and I, laughing, sat down at her piano and played "Heart and Soul," a simple duet, the only piece I can remember from my childhood lessons. I moved off the bench, and John started to play. As I watched his fingers fly across the keys, I imagined my mother there by his side, her hands poised to join in.

AGAINST THE ODDS

After Frances left, Miss Cooke arrived, the new governess for my brother Hap, now the adored baby of our family. To avoid her, I spent as much time as possible out of our house. Mostly, I gravitated down the block to the Metcalfs where I found a tenuous spot in their family between Lizzie, two years older, and Mary, two years younger. Nana Barletta, their nurse and a kind, loving French woman, understood my broken heart over Frances' departure and opened her arms to me.

Either I was in their basement reading Lizzie's impressive collection of comic books or outside in their playhouse where Mary and I would cook or clean or rock her dolls to sleep. The Metcalfs also had a television (banned in our house), and afternoons we were allowed to watch *The Mouseketeers* followed by *The Lone Ranger*. At 5 p.m. with a heavy heart, my loving, smiling Frances gone, I would head home.

At 10 years of age, I became a junior member of the California Tennis Club, the oldest private tennis club west of the Mississippi. I took some lessons from Dick Stevens, the pro, but had no friends to practice or play with. As soon as my half-hour lesson was over, I would rush to the bar and order a vanilla milkshake and a hamburger with fries and then watch anyone who was playing. I really wanted to join a clinic or go to any tennis camp anywhere, but my parents ignored my pleadings.

Afternoons when I was not at the Metcalfs, I would hit an old tennis ball against the uneven stone wall across the street from our house, stopping every few minutes to let a car go by. When I missed the ball and it soared into the heavy foliage, I would search diligently until I found it. Looking back on this lonely time, I realize this repetitive ritual kept my heart from being torn in two, and out of Miss Cooke's sights until dinner time.

In my mid-20's after the birth of my first son, I decided to take up tennis again and see if I could become a decent player, not an easy goal with no junior coaching or any tournaments under my belt. Oddly enough, tennis helped me countermand the turbulence in my life, physically centering me on a court with lines and rules, and mentally giving me the focus and discipline I would need later in my legal battles with my father.

With the help of Gil Howard, a gifted teacher, encouragement from Suzi, a talented tennis-playing friend who became my doubles partner, and Lloyd, a champion tournament player who kindly played mixed doubles with me, I improved and started playing local and club tournaments. Gil suggested I venture out to Golden Gate Park where many accomplished players gathered.

There I met Spencer Kern, 30 years older, who lived much of the time out of his 1950 blue Cadillac, the home of assorted wooden racquets, bizarre tennis outfits, and crumpled pizza boxes. When he asked me to play, I immediately accepted, eager to prove my prowess. On every crossover, he would sit on the bench and read a passage from Mary Baker Eddy while I stood, waiting, watching stray dogs wander through the courts. Bemused at first and confident of a win, I began to let everything irritate me, especially my resounding loss to Spencer.

In my early 30's, I signed up to play my first NorCal tournament, a Class C Category at Golden Gate Park that drew many good competitors. As I was waiting to be called for my match, I saw the #1 player in her age division warming up for her Class A match. "Bill," I said breathlessly, "that's *Arlene Cohen!*" Of course, she won her match handily, and I barely won mine, but I was thrilled nonetheless to watch her play and have my first significant win.

With his usual sense of humor, Bill couldn't wait to brag about my Class C victory, always eliciting the expected same response, "Who won A and B?" But when I began to win more tournaments, I gained credibility in his eyes, especially when three years later, he answered our phone and it was Arlene Cohen inviting me to play! Of course, I said yes. Since she was much better, I quickly realized she liked to play me so she could practice some aspect of her game. I never beat her either!

Over the years I played many club and NorCal tournaments and was graced with wonderful partners: Suzi Crary (my most formidable singles opponent); Lloyd Scott, who three times won the men's singles championship of the American Tennis Association; Bob Dalton, Cal basketball great who lead his team to win the NCAA basketball championship against the legendary Oscar

Robertson; Gil Howard, who won three Father-Son nationals with each of his sons; John Barry (member of New Zealand Davis Cup team); Charlie Hoeveler, winner of 52 national titles; Jim Farrell, a highly respected member of the San Francisco Police Department.

In September 1995 Jim Farrell and I entered the $5,000 Cal Club/Comerica Senior Tournament. In the semis we came up against the experienced team of Chuck and Chris Alloo. We split sets and then quickly got down 0-5, 0-40 in the third set. As Jim was about to serve, he turned to me and said, "Let's just get that ball over the net!" "Sounds good to me," I said. We ended up winning 7-5. Jerry Pang, tournament director and manager of the Cal Club, was later quoted in *Inside Tennis*. "I am still shaking my head. It was the most unbelievable comeback I've ever witnessed in tennis."

I had never heard of national tournaments—there are four each year for different age divisions—clay, grass, indoor, and hard court. At Suzi's urging, in 1985 we entered our first national tournament, the 40 Grass at Forest Hills. Although I had NorCal tournament wins under my belt, I still had a hard time believing in myself. Many times, when I stepped on the court to compete, I would ask myself, "What are YOU doing here?" There was always that inner voice I had a hard time silencing, questioning my abilities and whether or not I deserved to be there on the court.

Excited, Bill encouraged me to enter and said he'd love to join us—and even invite Ted, his older brother who lived in New York, to come down to watch. (By now Bill had stopped mentioning my Class C win!) We entered and learned (because of our NorCal ranking) we were seeded #3. When we read the draw, we couldn't believe how lucky we were to be playing in the first round an unseeded team, unknown to us, Bunny Smith and Mary McLean.

All I can say is by the time Bill's brother arrived to cheer us on, we were down 0-3 in the first set and never did win a game. We were literally wiped off the court in 40 minutes! Later we learned they had both played the circuit but were unseeded because they had no record together. A rude awakening to the world of national tennis, we got a taste of what it would take to win that elusive, most desired gold ball that is awarded for winning a national title.

Gil Howard, my wonderful coach, encouraged me to enter a Level 2 Tournament (one lower than a national), in Palm Springs at Mission Hills Country Club. I decided to enter all three events —singles, doubles, and mixed—and got to the finals in all three. Thrilled, I updated Bill, who told me to call after each one. After my singles loss, he said, "No worries, you still have two more events. Go get 'em!"

After I updated him on my doubles loss, he said, "Well, there's still the mixed." Then Gil and I lost that, and I couldn't bring myself to call Bill until we'd reached the airport. After being on a high to reach the three finals, I came home beyond discouraged. I remember this tournament so vividly because I realized in the competitive world of tennis, it's of no consequence if you reach the finals, even three of them, what people remember is who wins. I wondered then why I had set for myself such a seemingly unattainable goal of winning a national title. However, in retrospect, I feel these three back-to-back losses toughened my resolve to win a national title—to go for the gold.

Since I was raising three sons and also trying to pursue a writing career, I had to choose carefully what national tournaments I could play, usually only one a year, sometimes none. It wasn't until 1996, 11 years after the Forest Hills disaster, that I won my first ball, a bronze for third place in 50 singles, at the Chicago Indoors. I was beyond thrilled. Then in 1998 I won a bronze ball in 50 doubles there, and in 2001, I won my first silver ball as the finalist in 55 singles and another bronze in 55 doubles.

One tennis friend who has won over 55 gold balls throws out any bronze balls he has won, but I, on the other hand, will be forever proud and grateful for my first bronze ball. It was—for me—validation for all the hard work I had put into my tennis and gave me hope I could someday reach my goal, as distant as it seemed.

After my 2001 wins at Chicago Indoors, I gave the national tennis circuit a rest, but kept playing club and local tournaments. In 2005 I bumped into tennis great Charlie Hoeveler, who then asked me to play the National Indoor 60 mixed doubles in Seattle. I later learned he hadn't won his quota of gold balls that year and thought he could sneak up to Seattle and easily win the mixed—underestimating how tough the mixed draw would be.

Because I felt I was unprepared and not a good enough partner for him, I said I probably wouldn't be able to play. Later when I told Bill I had turned Charlie down, he remarked, "Linda, that is one of the stupidest things I've ever heard you say. You have to say yes. This is your chance to win a gold ball!" Gathering all my courage, I called Charlie and accepted his amazing offer, then immediately freaked out that I would let him down.

We did get to the finals but lost in straight sets to Ken Robinson and Mary Delay, seasoned players who had already won many gold balls. The weakest player on the court, I felt out of my league but was still thrilled to have won a silver ball. I could tell, however, that Charlie, always the gentleman, was disappointed. "Next year," he said, "We will have to come back and win."

True to his word, one year later he invited me to be his mixed partner at the Seattle 60 Indoors. This time, I was more prepared. We got to the finals and again our opponents were Ken and Mary. We split sets and were up 6-5 (my serve) in the third. All I had to do was win my serve, a tough task to say the least. We won 7-5. "You have your gold ball!" Charlie said, hugging me. In a state of total shock, I couldn't quite grasp that I had finally won what I had set my sights on 20 years earlier.

Running through the Seattle Airport to catch our plane, we passed a glass display of a pair of huge elephant tusks. Charlie turned to me and said, "I bet you are the *only* person in this entire airport, and United States, who has won a gold ball and also shot an elephant!" Most likely he was right.

After I broke my personal barrier, I returned the next year to the Vancouver Indoor Nationals and played mixed with David Bryant because Charlie was unavailable. We reached the finals, and again Ken and Mary were the opponents. And there I won my second gold ball. In 2010 Andi Polisky and I won the 65 women's doubles, and I was the finalist in singles.

Nine years after Charlie and I won Seattle, we entered the 70 mixed at the Asics tournament in Mission Hills, where I had lost all three finals. Now a national tournament for mixed doubles, we won it back to back for two years. Two months later, Bill died and I lost all interest in competing.

The following Christmas I thought, "Linda, you've got to get back on this horse. You can't give up your tennis." Out of the blue, the tournament director called me and said, "Frank Zebot needs a partner. He's great!" I didn't know him but decided to get back in the game. It's what Bill would have wanted. Frank and I met for the first time, just minutes before our first match, to discuss our strategy. He said, "I hope you play the ad court." I gulped. For the last few months, I'd only practiced from the deuce court and had never played the ad in a tournament. In addition, I hadn't executed a cross-court backhand groundstroke for a long time. But I answered, "No problem!"

Frank carried me through the week, and we prevailed in a very close final. I won my sixth gold ball. This would be, miraculously, my third consecutive victory for mixed doubles in this tournament. I know Bill was there, cheering for us all the way.

Had I not played tennis, I wonder how I would be faring today. Tennis has given me direction, hope, and a chance to rewrite my story with a positive ending. I have met many wonderful people through this sport who expanded my horizons and encouraged me to reach higher than I'd ever imagined. Tennis showed me the kind of person I could become with hard work and dedication. Miracles do happen!

INSPIRATION

PART IV

OTHERS TALK ABOUT THE AFTERLIFE

I believe there is no death, only a change of form from the physical to a rebirth into the life of the spirit. And from there our loved ones will help us as they did on earth. This knowledge that life continues after death has been a wonderful, healing tonic to ease my grief. The memories of Bill's life here, and the lives of all those who have touched my heart in love are never far from me.

Over the course of these past four years since Bill died, I began to share my experiences of Bill communicating with me from the beyond. In this section I present stories of friends who were also contacted by loved ones from the distant shore.

Animals can bring us so much joy in life, and we can feel their presence after they move on, as well. In this section, I include three stories about our beloved black Labradors—Shadow, Meg, and Sage.

TWO GRANDMOTHERS

BY KATIE SARGENT

Growing up as an only child, I was blessed to have both my maternal and paternal grandmothers very involved in my life. Since my paternal grandma was not close by, I would spend three weeks every summer with her, and we would also often talk on the phone. But in the last five years of her life, she lost her memory and had to live in an assisted-living home. When I would visit, she'd become agitated and angry; it was heartbreaking. I was devastated I couldn't make her last years happier and more comfortable.

As she was passing, my dad was at her bedside and called me on the phone. I could hear her breathing. I told her I loved her and had learned about determination and hard work from her. I also told her I hoped she would feel free and joyful now because I understood how trapped she'd felt at the facility. She died within the hour.

Two days later on a cold, foggy February day, I was with my

parents at my daughter's softball game. It was the first time she was pitching, and she was nervous. Suddenly, a huge and gorgeous yellow and black Monarch butterfly—certainly not the time of year to see one—buzzed me, then flew through the fence and made two loops around my daughter as she was walking out to the mound. It came back to me and then disappeared.

Several people in the stands asked, "Where in the world did that butterfly come from?" I turned to Mom and said, "Did you see that? I think it was Grandma." She agreed. Often when I am with Claire, my daughter, a black and yellow Monarch butterfly will appear. It's happened so frequently that we both say, "There she is!"

My grandmother loved to do needlepoint, and over the years had gifted me with seven of her treasures: a heart, a teddy bear, and finally, a big black and yellow Monarch butterfly. I know Grandma felt so trapped those final unhappy years of her life, and that she was using this butterfly to let us know that life for her now is wonderful, and that we shouldn't feel sad anymore.

Fifteen years after my other grandmother died, I fell sick with lymphoma. After each chemotherapy treatment, I would see an acupuncturist to manage the side effects. During one session I was feeling very sorry for myself—I was having an internal pity party. I'm young, I thought. I eat well. This is so unfair to my husband and my children. Why me?

Then I heard a voice I immediately recognized as my grandmother's softly say, "You know why." The acupuncturist turned and said, "Is there someone here in the room?" He looked around, saw nobody and returned to his work. No, I don't know why, I thought. And she said firmly, "Now you will know how much you are loved, and you will live your life in a better way."

I understood then she was encouraging me to be grateful and happy, not to wonder about what I didn't have, but appreciate how much I did. She made me see how I was surrounded by people who loved me and how important it was to find joy in my life every day.

With their communications from the other side, both grandmothers gave me precious gifts. I know now that nothing can end our love, no matter what form it comes in. And I also feel comforted knowing there is life after death.

HOPE IS A THING WITH FEATHERS

BY WENDY BINGHAM

My husband Dick and I often talked about what happens after we die. He promised he would never leave me. He would come back and somehow let me know he was by my side.

When Dick died, a close friend shared this dream: Dick was meeting with a council of angels, and they asked what form he wanted to take when he came back to earth.

"A bird," he said, "because I could fly back to my family and protect them."

Though I had never paid attention to birds, I began to look and listen. At my window appeared a cardinal—the first I'd ever seen. He seemed insecure, as if he didn't know how to work the feeder, but he learned and came back often. I knew then this was Dick's way of communicating with me.

A few months later, I was scheduled to play in a golf tournament. Walking down the hall at the club, I noticed all the garbage cans had cardinals on them. "Hi Dick," I said, as my partner approached, wearing a hat with a cardinal on it. Here was Dick again coming to reassure me.

I subscribe to an online prayer site, and recently found a picture of a cardinal, along with a story about parenting. Since my husband's death, I worried about how our 21-year-old twins were handling this devastating event. I had always looked to Dick for his wise counsel and advice.

As I read this story about how the greatest gift parents can give their children is to set an example of loving each other and also acknowledging that children are not our property, I heard Dick's voice. Once again, he was reminding me to let our girls spread their wings.

Recently I visited our summer home to plant some trees. When I arrived, I was shocked that our neighbors had cut down the hedge between our properties, the place where my new friend, the cardinal, liked to hide. Sobbing, I completely lost it—until I heard his familiar *chirp, chirp* nearby. Immediately I got Dick's message. "Come on, you can't accomplish anything being angry. Be strong. Forget the hedge. Go plant some trees."

At the nursery I chose two trees but couldn't decide on a third. Suddenly I saw the cardinal in the branches of a dogwood. Turning to the assistant, I said, "I'll take that one, too." Now hardly a day goes by that I don't see the cardinal.

One morning, after walking our dog, I came home and found the bird sitting quietly on a ledge above our kitchen sink. I panicked. What if I scare him and he flies into a window? Should I try to catch him in a towel? What if I injure him? All these feelings rushed through me. Then the cardinal gathered himself and calmly flew outside.

Yesterday I received a challenging email, one I knew I had to answer very carefully. I tried a few approaches. When I heard the cardinal's chirp I knew I was on the right track. This beautiful red bird is now a part of my life, reminding me that Dick is always nearby, guiding and loving me.

Later that day I saw, in Dick's study, a plaque I hadn't noticed before with a quote from Emily Dickinson: "Hope is a thing with feathers that perches in the soul and sings the song without the words and never stops at all."

I LOVE MY WIFE

BY NANCY ROSE

J ack and I shared a deep love of the outdoors. During our marriage we bought a beautiful piece of prime lakefront land on Lake Pend Oreille in northern Idaho where we hoped to build our dream home. But none of our kids were interested and the property sat undeveloped. For five years, Jack kept trying to convince me to sell but I dragged my heels. Finally, I listed the land and the realtor assured me it would sell immediately.

Soon thereafter, concerned about Jack's increasing weakness and forgetfulness, I went with him to the doctor. Handing Jack his prescription pad, Dr. A. directed him to write a sentence, any sentence. Slowly, Jack wrote, "I love my wife." When Jack couldn't answer a few simple questions, Dr. A. ordered an MRI. The results showed an inoperable brain tumor. Five months later, Jack died.

Devastated, I forgot about the property. Before Labor Day the realtor called to say he'd had no interest and was mystified. I decided to keep it on the market through the ski season. Then on September 25, Jack's birthday, the realtor called to say he had a fantastic offer, all cash, no contingencies. I knew immediately this was Jack's doing, that he was telling me to move forward and that when my day came, he would open his arms to me in our new home.

Jack and I had loved to travel, and retracing our steps from some of our trips abroad helped me cope with his loss. On June 26, 2016, the first anniversary of his death, I was in Bilboa, Spain, at the Guggenheim, one of our favorite museums. At the exact time he had passed, I walked out onto the terrace where a man stood holding a clarinet. When he saw me, he started playing "My Way," a song Jack had loved and often sung in the shower. Then he switched to *Ave Maria*, the song played at both my daughters' weddings as Jack, their stepfather, walked me down the aisle. Tears streaming down my cheeks, I knew absolutely that Jack was there, reminding me of his love.

Jack was especially fond of the English countryside. That September I found myself in Bibury, England, my first time there without Jack. Sad and missing him terribly, I decided to go into the St. Mary the Virgin Church. I knelt down and prayed to God and Jack for some sign that Jack was with me. After 20 minutes of feeling, hearing, and seeing nothing, I left the pew. Discouraged, I walked down the center aisle, still hoping.

Suddenly I was drawn to a funeral slab where I saw two names with two identical dates of death: Lucy Maria Baker, June 26, 1747, and Elizabeth Baker, June 26, 1747. June 26 was also the day Jack had died. I stood there for a long time processing this coincidence until my heart settled. I knew, however, without question he was letting me know of his love and he understood how much I was missing him.

The next year, in October, I attended my high school reunion in Tallahassee, Florida. As soon as the music started, I remembered all the fun times Jack and I had enjoyed on the dance floor. I had to leave before I broke down. The next morning, I made a teary visit to the Oakland cemetery, where Jack was buried. On the way, I was stopped at a long red light behind a black truck. I noticed a bumper sticker on its rear fender that said I LOVE MY WIFE. Since I had never seen one like that, I followed the truck and took a picture of it.

At my annual checkup with Dr. A, I asked if by some miracle he might still have the paper where Jack had written, "I love my wife." Reaching into Jack's file, he pulled out a small piece of white paper that I immediately recognized. I cried for joy.

Since then, there have been other occasions when Jack communicated with me from the other side. I am positive there is life after death and that I will be with Jack again. For now, I am comforted knowing he is watching over me, reminding me of his enduring love.

ENCOUNTERING ANGELS

BY ERICA JOUBERT

Do I believe in angels? Yes, yes, I do. They are around us every single day. When they are nearby, a light and a loving sensation comes through me. If I am in a down mood, I feel little touches on my cheek and arms. They guide and protect us. Also, I can see people who have died, a gift that is passed on through the women on my mother's side. My mother would talk of the angels all the time.

My first experience of an angel was when I was 13. I felt a presence and turned to see Nicki, my cousin who had died when I was 7. We had been very close. Standing in the doorway, she was wearing her usual white dress and her hair was in pigtails, tied with white ribbons. I couldn't believe what I was seeing, so I turned away, closed my eyes, and then looked back. She was still standing there. Then suddenly she was gone. For 6 years I had been worried she would never find me, but now I know that wherever I go, she will be nearby, wanting the best for me.

One day as I was leaving school, I saw a man looking at me from across the street. He had a cane. He was wearing grey pants, a red and black plaid shirt, and his black hair was parted on one side and slicked down. When I described him to my aunt, she explained he was my grandfather, a Blackfoot Indian, who had died before I was born, and that he was watching out for me.

Once at work I looked at my manager and saw a girl with reddish hair standing next to him. "How is the girl with red hair doing after her operation?" I asked. He was shocked. "That's my girlfriend, but I don't know how you know this." I answered, "The angels told me they want you to know that she'll be fine, but she must take it easy for a while."

Another time a woman came in to have a document notarized but I saw another being next to her demanding my attention. He wouldn't let me continue with my work until I passed on his message. "Tell her I know she is going through a hard time," he told me, "but that it will all work out. Let it flow and let it feel." When I relayed his words, the woman gasped and said, "My father always used to say that. What does this man look like?" I described his ocean blue eyes, his bald head on top with a fringe around it, and his outfit—blue jeans, tan belt, and a blue, white, and black flannel shirt. She started to cry. "That is the outfit my Dad wore all the time. Thank you, thank you for telling me this."

When Linda came to print this manuscript, I felt she was distressed. As she was about to leave, I said, "Wait, there is a man coming through; he's tall, has meat on his bones. He has dark brown hair, a prominent nose, and beautiful hazel eyes." She knew this was her husband Bill who had passed three years ago, and started to cry. "He wants you to know you have been blessed with many gifts," I added, "and that the people who are hurting you right now are blaming you for their own failures. They are jealous. Don't mind them. They are little; you are big."

The next day, Linda brought in a photograph of Bill in his youth. I said, "Yes. This is the man who came through to me. I have no doubt whatsoever. I believe that if I can see angels now they will be with me when it's time for me to cross that bridge. The same will be true for you."

A GREATER JOURNEY

BY KATHLEEN BRADY

Early one morning Ryan, 17, the oldest of my three sons, was driving to school with his youngest brother Keiler. Going 39 in a 25-mile per hour zone, he swerved to avoid a truck that had crossed into his lane. He remembered nothing afterwards, not their falling off an 80 foot cliff, hitting a tree that caused their car to flip six times to lodge between a retaining wall and the back deck of a house, not his hanging upside-down from the seatbelt with his elbow detached from his arm, not his brother holding it to stanch the bleeding, trails of blood dripping out the door.

Five fire departments coordinated the rescue operations, the hardest extraction they'd done in 30 years. One wrong move and the car would have crushed both boys. Waiting at the hospital for the ambulance to arrive, I heard a doctor yell, "Code Red, the brothers are coming."

The next day Ryan was hovering between life and death. He

later told me he saw my mother, his beloved Mei Mei, who had passed three years earlier, sitting near his right shoulder and wearing her favorite turquoise raincoat. She was offering him comfort and reassurance that he would recover.

An accomplished businesswoman and athlete, my mother infused our lives with her creative and joyful spirit. She always considered family her highest priority. Radiating unconditional love to all of us, she was very close to my three sons, especially Ryan, being the oldest. He will always remember her strong, unwavering presence on that critical day.

Ryan had a traumatic brain injury, numerous breaks in his neck and back, arm, clavicle, and elbow, and would need many surgeries. He then had to undergo intensive rehab to learn to speak and walk again. During this time Mei Mei came to him on three occasions, where he saw her floating nearby, smiling and happy, encouraging him to continue his healing. Throughout his year-long recovery, Ryan was always kind and positive, yet he was also aware of his part in the accident. Before that fateful day he had been a typical teenager who loved hanging out with his friends and wanted to spend a gap year in Spain before heading off to college. (He came out of his coma speaking Spanish!)

Today Ryan lives differently. He appreciates every moment and is deeply grateful for his recovery; he also thinks more about ways he can contribute to the lives of others. Just starting his first year at I.E. University, he has already been accepted for an internship for one of the top motivational podcasts. (He was the only one chosen out of 100 applicants.) He has also started his own website—studyabroadstudent.org—to help students navigate the visa process.

Ryan understands the importance of trying to be the best possible version of who he is, so he can bring light into this world and make the most of his second chance. Recently he said, "Mom, I know now without a doubt that my body goes but my sprit lives on." He understands, as do I, that there is more to our existence here on earth than what we can grasp with our five senses. Ryan and I are convinced that our consciousness doesn't end with death but continues on a much greater journey.

DAD'S RUN

BY NICK BUCKLIN

I t was August in our Montana camp, and I was 16. Although Dad had tried to interest me in fly fishing, I had not yet caught the bug. We walked together down to the river, and off I went exploring, as he, with Shadow by his side, headed upriver. As I was working my way back to camp, I saw him fishing one of his favorite stretches, one I could never quite understand why. To my inexperienced eye, it did not look particularly fishy. It was fast moving, had no pocket water, and was off a shallow bank with slippery, uneven rocks and swift currents.

"No way he'll catch anything there," I thought. "No one else has ever had any luck in this stretch of the river." When his rod bent, I realized he had hooked a fish. Here he was, in his twilight years with two fake knees, balancing precariously in his 20-year-old ripped wading boots, fighting a good-sized fish. I held my breath. After he landed it, a 16-inch Cutthroat, I waved and applauded. He freed the fish, then pointed to his fly and shouted, "Royal Wulff," flashing that wry smile I loved so much. While I had seen Dad catch countless fish over the years (never before, here), these 15 minutes are etched in my memory. I named this spot Dad's Run.

By my early 20's, I became hooked on fly fishing and would return many times to fish this run, always with no success. Each failed attempt reinforced my long-held belief that it was unproductive water, and Dad had just been extremely lucky that August day when I was 16. Now it was August again, and I was 33. Mom, Christian, John, and I were gathered together in our Montana camp to spread Dad's ashes. Before going to the top of the hill, his favorite place, I decided to try Dad's Run one more time. Past experience had trained me to be pessimistic, and I knew I had little chance of catching a fish, but as every angler can attest, there's always the chance…and besides, I was doing it in Dad's honor.

I tied on a Royal Wulff and fished his run for 30 minutes, more time than I'd otherwise dedicate to a regular, unproductive stretch of water. Cocktail time was approaching, and I needed to meet the others at camp. I cast once more and then turned to start my trek back to shore. I felt the line go tight. I went from scrambling on a rock and looking in the wrong direction to fish on mode. My heart raced. I could not lose this fish. Stripping in the slack line, I managed to land it. There he was, all 16 inches of native Cutthroat trout with a large jaw and bright red signature markings. Strong and sturdy, just like Dad.

After Dad's death I was not only overcome with grief but also with uncertainty. I had lots of questions and precious few answers. Many of life's big decisions felt daunting; Dad, the person who had always reassured me, was no longer here to guide me. That day I knew for certain that Dad was there, watching me catch that fish, cheering me on, and celebrating our shared love for each other and of fishing.

COMPANIONS ON THE JOURNEY

PART V

SUNLIGHT AND SHADOW

R ivers are woven into the story of my life, their light and shadows pierce my soul, drawing me to what lies below their surface beauty, to what I can't see but only imagine. This yearning to explore the depths plays out throughout my life. We all have rivers of our own, separate ones that carry us forward, but ones that begin and end together.

Two small rivers graced our family's ranch in Northern California. These waters of my youth wrapped themselves around my heart, and after we lost the ranch, I searched elsewhere to find a replacement. Bill and I began spending summers in Montana, where we would camp by the North Fork of the Blackfoot River. I heard its call and couldn't resist running to its side. I loved its sparse, deep pools, eddies, and rushing riffles, its clean mineral smell mixed with mint and pine.

Alone in camp one day with Shadow, our beloved black Labrador, I thought of my sweet mother. Sitting down to read

Little Rivers by Margot Page, I came to the part when her mother is dying. Margot sits next to her, holding her hand in the darkness of her bedroom, when her stiff-upper-lip Yankee mother says, in a voice choked with pain, "I'll miss helping you with your babies."

I cried, remembering how much I had yearned for my mother to witness and cherish me as a mother to my three sons. But she died two years before Christian, my first, was born. As I wept, Shadow, my little black angel, an old dog full of aches and pains, awakened and put her head on my lap, then licked my hands and legs. For a long while she stayed close to me, her wise brown eyes never leaving mine. My heart settled. Many times since her passing, Shadow has eased my loneliness. I can feel her loving presence in my dreams.

THE DOG WHO NEVER STOPPED WAITING

Our front door is framed on either side by a panel of windows which give Sage, my three-year-old lab, a world view of what's going on outside. Perched on her pad, she barks her hellos to anyone walking by with a dog—which is almost everyone! An experienced voyeur, she saves her loudest ones for Stanley, a handsome big black lab, and Rocky, her black and white springer spaniel neighbor across the street.

After Bill died, every morning after breakfast Meg, his beloved 15-year-old lab and Sage, then an eager, naughty juvenile, would set up watch in the front hall. There they would wait patiently for him, Meg occasionally jostling Sage to get a better view of his grey Subaru parked in the driveway. After a time Sage would come find me, but until it was time for a walk or a meal, Meg never left her post.

Her determination to be together with him again, to sit at his side, and look up into his eyes, her need to feel his hand run over her back was unwavering. Before Bill died, mornings she would wait on her pad until he arose, and I would come to help her up, her back legs frozen from age and arthritis. But now with Bill gone, she would get up on her own, stiffly following me to the kitchen and later outside, before settling in to wait for her master's return.

Often she was incontinent, and her pace slowed, but she still managed to get around. She never gave up hope. Finally, I called the vet, and we agreed Meg's time had come. Born on May 8, 2001, at 15 years plus, she had lived a long and wonderful life. On July 15, 2016, the vet came to my home, and we gathered in the back yard. John and I held Meg, who had difficulty now raising her head.

Over and over again, we told her what a good and loyal girl she was, how she had retrieved more ducks than Shadow did, and how she would soon be with her one and only Bill. When she heard us whisper "Bill," her ears moved. She sighed and settled down into my arms. And then, only then, did she let go of her place on this earth, the light dimming in her dark brown eyes.

I know they are together now. I have dreams of them at the beach, Bill, in a ripped t-shirt and faded madras bathing trunks, his curly hair unruly, and Meg, muscles taut, waiting expectantly by his side. I watch as he cocks his arm and throws a ball. Meg takes off like a flash, running like the wind, eager to please the master she loves.

FINDING SAGE

The day after Meg passed, John took Sage, now an only child, for a long hike to the ridge of Big Rock, an area unfamiliar to Sage. It was an extremely hot July day. For some reason—perhaps drawn to the scent of a deer or fox—Sage ran off into a ravine and never returned. John spent hours calling and searching for her, then alerted the Ranger Station she was missing.

Everyone in the area helped us look for her. John put up flyers, retraced his steps, never stopped calling for her. Pinkie, my dear friend, suggested we camp out in the ranger parking area where John and Sage had started their hike, and barbeque in the hope of enticing her back. Nick and I hiked and called. We all worried how a small year-old female lab could survive in this wilderness of suffocating heat, large rattlesnakes, dried up streams, coyotes, and the odd mountain lion.

The first evening after we barbecued, John set up his sleeping bag in the back of his truck. When I arrived the next morning, he'd already hiked all over their route with no sign of Sage. "I heard a pack of coyotes howling and yipping in the hills last night," he told me. "They were out hunting." My heart was in my throat, and I felt like throwing up. "Let's keep on searching," I said.

The rangers generously helped us. They drove their six-wheeler over much of the terrain hoping to catch a sighting. By afternoon we were discouraged but not ready to give up. John cooked hamburgers. "If we don't find Sage tomorrow, then I think another night here is a waste of time," I said. John agreed. We sat in silence and watched the sky fill with stars. I left as he was settling down in the back of his truck for another long night.

Arriving back in Mill Valley, I heard the phone ring. "Hello?" I said. "Have you found your dog yet?" questioned an unfamiliar voice. "No," I said. "Well, I hope you find her soon. I just saw a pack of fourteen coyotes near the trailhead."

Numb, I hung up. Four months earlier Bill had died, and the day before, Meg had as well. Now I was faced with the probability of losing Sage. I didn't know if I was strong enough to handle this. I took an Ambien and fell into a dreamless sleep.

Early the next morning I was awakened by the sound of the front door opening and then sharp click-clicks on the hardwood floors. The clicking grew closer. Disoriented, not daring to hope, I sat up and there was Sage. It still didn't sink into my consciousness that she was home, but then she jumped on my bed and started licking my face. I wrapped my arms around her, never wanting to let her go.

"Mom," John said. "The entire night there were coyotes

milling around the parking lot. I would shine my flashlight, and all I could see were pairs of red eyes. They circled my truck. Nothing scared them. But then just at dawn I felt the truck move, and suddenly there was Sage, who had jumped up onto my sleeping bag. She was breathing hard and highly agitated."

A few days later I told a friend this story and said I felt it was a miracle that Sage had returned unharmed to us. She said, "You know, Linda, there is a belief in the Japanese culture that when a dog who has been greatly loved by a family dies, it wants to thank that family for their love. The dog's way of showing appreciation is to carry away one misfortune that would have fallen on the family."

As soon as she told me this story, I knew beyond knowing that this is what happened to us. Meg, who had died the day before Sage went missing, kept Sage safe those hot days and dark nights she was alone in the wilderness and led her back to us. This was Meg's gift, her way of saying, "Thank you for loving me so much."

TAKING TIME TO REMEMBER

Being alone during the coronavirus lockdown has given me greater perspective on what is important and what I can do without. Before this challenging time, I filled my day with exercise, phone calls, appointments, lunches, and other social activities, leaving little time for introspection. These days I have nothing on my calendar and ample time for my thoughts and feelings to roam.

Now I pay more attention to the small moments, moments when I visualize my wonderful family and dear friends, silently thanking them with my heart for their loving kindness; moments of beauty as I watch a hummingbird hover over the blossoms on my lemon bush; moments of joy when I dance to "Saturday Night Fever;" "aha!" moments when I read a poem by Mary Oliver; peaceful moments when I clip the ends of pale peach roses and arrange them with white freesias in my favorite glass vase; moments of grace when I thank God and all the angels surrounding us for their unconditional love and guidance.

And I cherish the moments when Sage, my faithful Lab, comes to rest her head on my knee. An irreplaceable comfort, especially during this isolation, she is never far from my side, a reminder of all the pets I have loved. I have time now to remember.

When I was three, my nurse Frances gave me two lovable parakeets, one yellow and one blue. They were tame enough to sit on my shoulders and they accompanied me wherever I went in our cavernous house. When I danced to music Frances would play on the phonograph, they sat on my head and kept their balance, and I could feel their tiny feet scratching my scalp. When I sat in my highchair in the kitchen, they would walk up and down my chubby arms. I also had a miniature turtle with the Golden Gate Bridge painted on his back, but his stay in my room was short-lived.

We had a number of other pets all belonging to Mom, who shared the wealth: a bouncy, black standard poodle, Zibilene, Zibby for short, along with a sneaky, independent Siamese cat named Pyewacket. Early mornings Pye would climb up our fire escape, slide through an open window, creep into my parents' bedroom, then settle down on Dad's chest to eat a sparrow he'd caught. Mom would awaken to a symphony of Dad's snores and the crunching of tiny bones. Sinka, another Siamese, joined our menagerie, and soon found his place under my covers at night, away from Zibby, curled on top.

One Christmas my godmother gave me a fancy, leather-bound manicure set that my mother instructed me to guard with my life. One day, after proudly showing it to a friend, I left it on my desk. Always on the prowl, Sinka jumped up and sharpened his claws on the smooth, rich surface of the case. Devastated, I hid it in my drawer. But Miss Cooke, my younger brother's nurse, showed it to my mother. When I explained what happened, Mom didn't believe me and sent me to my room "to think about the importance of telling the truth." Just days later Mom found Sinka on top of her bureau ripping up a silk jewelry case and realized she'd misjudged me.

Pepe, a large standard poodle, came next, along with Cocie, a beautiful, dark brown Burmese cat who loved my mother and slept on the pillow next to her. Then there was Sebastian, Dad's black lab, his prized hunting dog, who had to stay in the basement in a kennel with an outdoor, cement run. In those days hunters held the belief that if a retriever lived indoors, he would become too soft. Only during summers at the ranch would Sabe be free from his kennel.

One night in San Francisco, however, after a wine-filled dinner, Dad asked Adrian, the butler, to bring Sabe upstairs. Beyond excited to see his master, Sabe couldn't stop wagging his thick tail, soon leaving spatters of blood from the tip he'd torn in his exuberance everywhere, especially on the white living room couch and chairs. He was never allowed upstairs again. My heart aching, I would sneak down to visit him, rubbing his soft ears and strong chest.

At the ranch we all roamed free throughout our immense garden. Because of the heat Sabe and Pepe chose to stay on the porch under the overhang, but I would see Sinka everywhere, slinking through the orchards, branches heavy with peaches and plums, hiding in the tendrils of the grape arbor surrounding our swimming pool, or sneaking among the lemon bushes, on constant alert for lizards. Mom would always be in her rose garden with our houseboy Gee nearby. He often used his hoe to chop off the head of a rattlesnake that had crossed their path.

There was a resident king snake, the mortal enemy of the rattlesnake, that lived year-round somewhere near the roses. One lazy afternoon we heard what sounded like a broken sprinkler—rat-ta-tat-rat-ta-tat-tat-tat—and discovered Sinka in battle mode against a rattlesnake he had cornered. Fortunately, Mom persuaded him to back off, and the large snake slid away. We all hoped the king snake was nearby.

Over the years of our marriage, Bill and I shared our home with four wonderful dogs—a golden retriever first, with three labs following. My favorite Lab was Shadow, the runt of the litter, that we took reluctantly when we found out the puppy we'd chosen had been mistakenly sold. Small yet emotionally the most intelligent member of our family, she would edge her way onto our couch, then hop up and quietly drape herself around Bill's shoulders.

We had other assorted pets, our least favorites being two of Nick's choices: a baby rat "Ratsy" that quickly grew into a large one with a long tail and a sizable turtle "Fred" that did nothing but run up vet bills and eat mealworms I'd find in Nick's couch. Christian had a delightful hamster "Hampy" that was quite tame and sat with us when we had cocktails, until he jumped off my lap and disappeared. Distraught, we looked everywhere; one month later he reappeared, fat and happy, from under the top floor couch where we all watched TV, often with snacks in hand.

Our favorite was a peach-faced lovebird that happened to fly through a window and land, exhausted, near John. We had never seen such a beautiful little bird—bright green feathers with an orange head and neck fringed with peach fuzz. He even had a peacock blue tail feather. Tame, needy, and noisy, he immediately made himself at home. Nights when we watched the news, he would munch on our earlobes. Happily chattering away, he would fly off to swing from a curtain, then zoom over to sit on the top of our golden retriever's head. Only when we covered his cage at night would he be silent.

I'm grateful for the joy and merriment these pets have brought me. Through my childhood, they helped me laugh and taught me personal responsibility. When I was three, Frances asked me what I wanted to be when I grew up. I said, "I want to be a mother cat with kittens."

Memories are gifts from the afterlife. During these days of quarantine, I feel their presence and know that I am not alone. Armed with these images, and with Sage by my side, I will carry on during these uncertain times. When I venture outside, I wear one of Bill's red plaid cowboy handkerchiefs as the required facemask and I feel his strong hand holding mine.

EPILOGUE

THE JOURNEY CONTINUES

After Dad died, my stepmother Denise kindly gave me a packet of over 55 letters tied with white string she had found tucked far back in the corner of a shelf in his dressing room. With the exception of two from my father, I discovered the rest were all letters my mother had written to him in the summer of 1933. Just 21 and a graduate of Stanford, she was taking a three-month tour from San Francisco to Europe and back. At 23 Dad was going to summer school to prepare for Stanford Law School in the fall.

On a short leash financially, he spent much of his time in college playing poker to make ends meet (which left him little time for his studies). As the story goes, Dad heard Mom was considered one of the smartest girls on campus. Both were in the same English seminar, both had papers due, and he hadn't started his. Inviting Mom on a canoe ride, he casually suggested she bring along her paper. When they were in the middle of the lake, he asked to see it. Standing up to hand it to my overeager father, she tipped the canoe, and they fell, pages and all, into the lake. After this drenching, a romance began, sparking a marriage that lasted 33 years.

Until the last few years of their marriage, I had always thought my parents were a love match, one that was destined; I worried I wouldn't be able to find that someone meant just for me. But when Mom died, I couldn't erase the destructive acts of Dad's cruel behavior that had contributed to her ending her life. And I couldn't understand her unwavering loyalty to him. My view of their marriage was shattered. These letters swept me into their world of young love, and I began to wonder why Dad had kept them for 63 years. Maybe he'd forgotten they existed. Or maybe their presence reassured him that my mother loved him just for his heart and soul. Whatever the scenario, I believe now they are in the Light, and all is forgiven.

July 6, 1933

My darling,

A very strange combination of emotions seems to be mine for tonight. I have dreaded making final arrangements for this trip, knowing that it meant leaving you—and yet on top of all the choking sadness, I am really very happy—because you talked to me tonight and told me just the things that will carry me through. I love you so very dearly—depend on you and need you, that I am not successful in even trying to manage without you. But we have a perfect understanding that is helping us—knowing that anything could happen and we could still work it out together. We have an everlasting trust and a mutual respect—all this and

loads more to balance our love. Should two people ever fail,
having everything?
With all my dearest love,
Pat

July 8, 1933
Darling, It is even worse missing you than I imagined it would
be. Going out under the Golden Gate was beautiful, but heartbreaking. I hope I never feel again the way I did when I stood
there waving goodbye to you. I am never going away again and
leave everything (you) behind the way I have this time. I stood
waving so long that I missed half of dinner. Lonesomeness for
you keeps just rushing over me in waves. I no sooner get over
one attack than another one commences. The perfect faith I have
with you makes everything all right.
With all my dearest love,
Pat

July 18, 1933
Darling, tragedy has overtaken us—and at this point we are
wandering aimlessly around the Pacific—some thousands of
miles due south of Chicago, forty miles off the coast of Central
America. The engines died at 10:30 this evening, and the whole
crew is frantic. Everyone has been jittering around, and just
before midnight, Wallie and I decided to go swimming. We
looked as though we'd been painted with radium, there was so
much phosphorus in the pool. Every move we made left long
streaks and bubbles of light. The stars are so close to us I could
reach up and gather a whole handful and bring them home to

you. Good night, sweet, and love me because I love you to death.
Lovingly,
Pat

August 1, 1933
Tonight the Professor and his wife gave a bridge party for Wallie and me in their cabin. I kept wishing all night you could see us. Their cabin is small, and it ended up with me seated in the bathroom and visible to no one except Wallie. We told the captain about this, and he, having a good old Norwegian sent of humor, said, "How convenient to get on the toilet and play bridge at the same time!" There was a whole room full of people who heard his remark and were highly embarrassed. It is late now, sweet, and I am going to say goodnight—and God bless you, and I love you. It takes me ages to write you, because I continually interrupt myself by thinking about you and us and how marvelous I will feel when I see you again.
Lovingly,
Pat

With my mother's letters was this response from my father.

August 30,1933
Dearest,
When any little thing goes wrong, then I find how much I really need you. I did not realize until you went away how happy you sure make me when I am blue. Just seeing you seems to dispel all my troubles and I am again happy. Oh, darling, if you only knew

how much I depend on you to help me get the things from life that make it so worthwhile. I don't suppose I should wear my heart so on my sleeve for you will probably go get yourself another man, feeling you can always come back to me. Although you would be more than welcome, I am afraid I would be too heartbroken to help you much. I am really terribly sad, going away to Shasta. If you were going, then I would be the happiest young fellow in all this world. Please take good care of yourself for me and darling, do hurry and come home. I am getting more anxious every day. I shall probably be a jittering wreck when you do come. I can hardly wait to see you, and I only hope you are as glad to see me. Please love me, darling, and take awful good care of yourself.

Goodbye and all my love, pumpkin.

Prentis

On a recent family camping trip in Montana, I was comforted, thinking of my parents' letters, and the love that was once at the core of their marriage. When I shared the contents with my sons, they were deeply moved. The only story they had heard was all about my mother's unhappiness.

One dark, moonless night John awakened me. "Mom, I see what looks like a comet below the Big Dipper." Setting up his camera, he took many photos of what we would find out in the morning was the Neowise Comet, discovered two months earlier. The next time this comet would be visible to earth was 6,800 years from now. Deep in my heart I hoped this was truly the harbinger of new wisdom and rebirth for our troubled planet.

Our final night in camp I hosted a gathering for cherished Montana friends. After dinner John lit a fire, and we talked and laughed until the sky was dark and blanketed in stars. Close to midnight John pointed out the Neowise Comet, and we again delighted in its beauty. We are all souls making our way back to the same source. On earth we are confronted with difficulties, opportunities, decisions, each one defining our yearning for wholeness. As I struggle with how this plays out for me in everyday life, I always come back to love.

Here in our Montana camp, my life is simple, a far cry from the privileged, power-driven one of my youth, but one filled with special moments: sharing stories and laughing with my three wonderful sons, sitting behind John as he paints a plein air scene, touching shoulders with Christian as we look out at the rugged mountains, watching Nick gracefully cast his fly over Bill's favorite stretch of the North Fork.

One day I hiked with John to Glacier Lake, at 7,000 feet, an emerald jewel surrounded by snow-covered peaks. I was scared to cross a log hanging over swollen, rushing waters that had already wiped out a portion of the trail. Sage pushed ahead and ran to other side. My heart was pounding, but with John's encouragement, I inched across. When we got to a second, more perilous log, I balked. John said, "Mom, we've come this far. We can't turn back." Then he found a calmer place where we could ford the river and pick up the path on the other side. Hiking back through fragrant huckleberry bushes, bear grass and purple lupin, I was thrilled to have found the courage to keep on going.

On the same vacation, a fishing guide took us down the Missouri River, and I caught a 20 inch Rainbow trout on a tiny fly called an elk hair caddis. I hiked with Sage whose joyful exuberance led me through juniper and pine, and endured mercurial weather—days of cold rain and fierce winds blowing through my tent. Once I spent six hours in my sleeping bag, Sage by my side, wearing my warmest clothes to stop my shivers.

There were bluebird days and evenings when a stillness settled over the landscape. On top of the hill where we had spread Bill's ashes, Nick spotted a smooth granite rock. Picking it up, he discovered it was a snapping turtle keeping watch over tiny eggs beneath her. Carefully, he placed her back on her nest, knowing that after being touched, she might not stay. "Way to go, Nick," laughed Christian. When we returned the next evening, the eggs had hatched, small white pieces of shell the only evidence of this miracle.

I loved spending evenings in camp with my three sons, seated around the simple, wooden table John had built, with a half-filled bottle of Bighorn Bourbon, a bouquet of Indian paintbrush, lupin, and daisies, eating scoops of huckleberry ice cream. Christian, John and Nick told stories—who climbed highest that day, who caught the biggest fish, who saw the most elk—each one trying to outdo the other. Sage would sneak off to her own cot next to mine on the tent porch, keeping watch, her beautiful amber eyes shining in the dark.

On occasion we had dinner with beloved Montana friends, whose warmth and open arms settled my anxious heart and gave me a sense of belonging. Always I felt Bill nearby, celebrating our happiness.

Since Bill passed over, there have been several special events I wish he could have witnessed with me. *The Love of Angels*, my third book that contains a story by him, was published. Lucas, my fourth grandchild, was born, and to my delight he resembled Bill. I won my sixth national tennis championship, attained Life Master status in duplicate bridge, traveled to Normandy to play on the US tennis team against France, and recently was a finalist in the National 75 Mixed Doubles in Palm Springs.

In addition to these happy times, there were some dark ones. Meg died. The caregiver who had briefly helped me when Bill was dying robbed me. I took a disastrous fall on the tennis court, smashing my collarbone and bruising the entire left side of my body. It took a year to recover. Sage was lost in the wilderness for three days and later nearly died of an infection. And I fell sick, only to discover I had pneumonia in my left lung, the same diagnosis Bill had received before dying.

During these difficult days, my family and close friends were of great support. Thanks to them and to Bill's guiding messages from the other side, I keep on saying yes to life. I enjoy watching Christian as he embarks on a new business venture, John as he creates yet another beautiful painting, and Nick as he puts his MBA and CFA to good use in the business world. I cheer Katie as the lead singer in an all-male band and Sam at his many baseball games. I hold Sophia and Lucas close to my heart as I read them *The Story of Babar: The Little Elephant* at bedtime.

I embrace my loved ones who are no longer here, especially my parents. "I know," I say softly to my mother, "that you never stopped loving us." And to my father I say, "Maybe now you understand why I had to venture into the wilderness and challenge you. And perhaps, too, you realize I never stopped loving you."

In writing this book, I see more clearly that life is a journey, and it takes years to understand all the twists and turns of our path. We choose this incarnation because there are things we need to learn and accomplish here. While it's not always possible to work through all our issues in one lifetime, it's important to confront what we are called to face. And if we fill our life with things and endless action, when will we have time to make that long slow journey across the desert to follow our guiding star and discover what lies beyond this earth?

Recently, I discovered Laura Lynne Jackson's wonderful book, *The Light Between Us.* A psychic medium, she has dedicated her life to exploring our connections to the Other Side, writing of her many conversations with loved ones who have passed over. She urges us to open ourselves to the possibility of life after death, to experience this light-filled connection we all have the opportunity to share. Throughout her book she describes vibrant cords of light that tie us to those we love, that can never be broken even when we cross.

In praise of her book, Dr. Eben Alexander, M.D., author of *Proof of Heaven*, writes: "Laura Lynne Jackson's personal story is beautifully wrought. She weaves together the extreme challenge of the scientific proof of mediumship with the profound healing aspects of love and the overwhelming evidence for the eternity of our souls and their connections."

One recent evening, I didn't want to put down *The Light Between Us* and fell asleep with the book open. Later that night my phone rang once, waking me. Startled, I found myself sitting up in bed with the book open, light still on. I looked at my cell phone (normally in the kitchen or my study) to see if any family had called (no one had) and saw the time was 11:11 P.M. For Bill and me, that particular time had held a special meaning, a sign of love and spiritual connection. Whenever we were together and would see this time, we would reach out to hold hands.

"The Trapped Bee" is the story of Charlie and RoseAnn, a New York City couple, who'd had a reading with Laura Lynne. As she began, she saw they'd been married a long time and had no children. Then a point of light appeared on her screen that was a big, black dog with an S name. "Oh," the couple exclaimed. "That was our first dog Shadow, a Doberman-Lab mix."

More and more points of light came through during the session, different animals, dogs, cats, sparrows, ducklings, a tortoise, even a tiny bee, that Charlie and RoseAnn had rescued or cared for over the years. Laura Lynne explained that when our animals cross, they are happy and pain-free, "romping through fields, flying through skies, swimming through reefs, and thanking us for all the love we gave them when they were here. We will see them again."

Dr. Kenneth Ring, professor emeritus of psychology at University of Connecticut and one of the leading scholars in the field of Near Death Experiences, describes mystical or transcendent experiences reported by people who have been on the threshold of death. In his amazing book, *Lessons from the Light*, he concludes that we need not fear death because "what we encounter will be beautiful, more beautiful than words can express. The truth is, we are connected to another world."

These days, I take comfort in reading about near-death experiences and accounts of psychic mediums' readings. They describe the beauty and light of the world beyond, making the case that our consciousness survives the physical realm, and that when we pass to the Other Side, we will again be connected with our loved ones who are waiting for us.

I understand now that our greatest strength is our capacity to love and forgive. Only love has the power to heal and reunite us with our true selves and with others, and always, love will carry us home.

As I am finishing this book in April, I have a session with an Intuitive who tells me that my mother is present and eager to communicate. "She is holding a rose," the Intuitive says, "and she wants you to have it." (My mother and I shared a special love of roses.)

"Your mother tells me that on earth she was more focused on your sister and older brother. She didn't worry about you because you were like a cat that lands on its feet. Now she really wants to spend more time with you."

The Intuitive has other messages from her as well. "She is watching you pass the torch and happy you understand what family means. She is proud you are such an amazing mother. Your sons know how much you love them, yet also appreciate that you have encouraged them be independent.

"Your mother loves you very much. She keeps saying Happy Birthday, not this month, but next month." I was surprised by the accuracy of this Intuitive. My birthday is in fact May 12.

When I ask about Bill, the Intuitive says, "Oh yes, your husband is here, too. He's a very strong presence. He's smiling, there's a twinkle in his eye and he is holding a bouquet of white lilies." (These flowers were our favorites.)

"He is very svelte and handsome now—not the way he was before he passed. He is mentioning a country Western singer you both love. And he wants you to look for a belt buckle with the American flag on it that has something to do with eagles. He says you will find it in the top drawer of his bureau. He loves you very much and knows you love him, too. And he is proud of your new book."

She continues: "Your husband insists that you need to be more open to accepting help. You've accomplished so much already and now he wants you to enjoy life. He is telling me you still have an abundant time on earth and hopes you will have another heart connection."

When I hear this, I start weeping, telling the Intuitive I don't want to be here that much longer because I miss Bill. She answers with "Hold your horses," a phrase he used often, and I know that Bill is aware of my grief and asking me to be open to new experiences.

After our session ends, I open Bill's top bureau drawer and find a small box holding a 2015 commemorative belt buckle for the NRA Golden Eagles, a limited edition that he treasured. Later I listen to Willie Nelson's "Always on my Mind," the song Bill first used to tell me he was nearby.

Love is everything. Someday I will once again become one with the Light, and Bill will be there waiting for me. My journey continues toward the distant shore.

THE LOVE OF ANGELS

From a young age, I have believed in the existence of angels. Certainly no expert, I just knew they were there for me and for everyone. I see them as spiritual beings, highly conscious guides, who love us and want only the best for us. Gary Quinn explains in his wonderful book, *May the Angels Be with You*, that angels are also messengers, "the wires of the universe—they afford us a means of spiritual communication...They can be people we've loved on this earth who have passed over, or they can be spiritual beings we haven't known."

Appearing in any form God decides, they can communicate with us through a song, a fragrance, a verbal suggestion, a commanding voice or a dream. With powers and abilities far beyond ours, they lead us to a greater understanding of our own capacity to love; they also help us see how transformative the power of love can be. For me, angels can also be people—strangers, family, and friends—whose lives have touched mine in this life, whose loving actions have opened up my heart to greater love and understanding. I place animals in this category as well.

Years ago at a low point in my life, I had a powerful dream of being with angels. They were showing me paintings I had done that were hung throughout an immense room. I was particularly drawn to one on the ceiling of two angels looking downwards. Then I felt many arms cradling me as one would cradle a baby. When I awoke, I was filled with a sense of love and security. That dream gave me strength to continue, with firmer steps, on a path that was both painful and challenging.

In a recent move, I reconnected with an old friend who for many years had been a tennis partner and opponent. We delighted in our "new" friendship; we began playing bridge together and shared tennis stories and pictures of our families. One day at the bridge center, she noticed I was holding Eben Alexander's *Proof of Heaven;* taking a quick look, she turned to me and said forcefully, "Linda, how can you be so naïve as to think that there is anything or anybody beyond this life now?" Stunned, I said, "It's a wonderful book. You should read it." Shaking her head, she just laughed.

One week later she got the terrible news she had terminal cancer that had spread so quickly she had only weeks to live. When I went to visit, Hospice was there, and she was already going in and out of consciousness. Holding her limp hand, I started talking. "Joan, you are surrounded by love. You are not alone. You are beloved." She squeezed my hand; her eyes opened, and she smiled. "Linda, you make me feel so wonderful, so happy." Then she drifted off. I stayed with her for a long time telling her about God and angels and how she would be lifted home with love.

Two days later on a crystal clear, windless morning, I was playing tennis. My opponents were taking a break, and I was standing near the net. Suddenly, out of nowhere, a gauzy, wispy cloud appeared in front of me and stayed there for over five minutes, hovering, not dissipating. Right then I knew beyond knowing it was Joan coming to reassure me that she now understood she was in the arms of angels and that I shouldn't worry. She died the next morning.

The Love of Angels includes my own stories and those of others who have shared their encounters with loving beings. It is my hope that these stories will lift our hearts and be reminders of our connection to the Divine. The word angel means messenger in both Greek and Arabic. Aren't we all messengers, sending a message to those around us through the lives we lead? Thomas Merton wrote, "Because we love, God is present." Living our lives in love is what carries us onwards in our journey home to the light on that distant shore.

Available in Paperback and eBook from Your Favorite Bookstore or Online Retailer

RECOMMENDED READING

Wired for High Level Wellness: Simple Ways to Rejuvenate, Meditate & Prosper, Susan Smith Jones, PhD, Books to UPLIFT, 2020

Appointments With Heaven, Dr. Reggie Anderson, Tyndale House Publishers, 2013

Proof of Heaven, Eben Alexander, M.D., Simon and Schuster, 2012

To Heaven and Back, Mary C. Neal, M.D., Waterbrook Press, 2011

Forever, Mildred Crum, Alfred A. Knopf, 1942
Daring Greatly, Brene Brown, PhD, LMSW, Gotham Books, 2012

Braving the Wilderness, Brene Brown, PhD, LMSW, Random House, 2017

The Light Between Us, Laura Lynne Jackson, Spiegel & Grove, 2016

Letters From the Light, Written Through the Hand of Elsa Barker, Beyond Words Publishing, 1995
Talking to Heaven, James Van rage, Dutton, 1997

Only Love is Real, Brian L. Weiss, M.D., Warner Books, 1997

What Happens When We Die, Echo Bodine, New World Library, 2013

Life After Death, Mary T. Browne, Ivy Books, 1994
God and the Afterlife, Jeffrey Long, M.D. with Paul Perry, HarperOne, 2016

Embraced by the Light, Betty J. Eadie, Gold Leaf Press, 1992

Emmanuel's Book, Compiled by Pat Rodegast and Judith Stanton, Bantam 1987

Surviving Death, Leslie Kean, Crown Archetype, 2017
The Path of the Soul, White Eagle, White Eagle Publishing, 1959

Edgar Cayce on Prophecy, Mary Ellen Carter, Paperback Library, 1968

ACKNOWLEDGMENTS

My deep gratitude to the following writers and witnesses to my life:

Valerie Andrews, whose gifted editing and guidance were invaluable

Susan Smith Jones, whose encouragement of this book lifted it to another level

Mary Keil, my champion, whose creative talents have always been beacons of inspiration

I would also like to thank Kathleen Brady, Nick Bucklin, Wendy Bingham, Erica Joubert, Nancy Rose, and Katie Sargent for sharing their wonderful stories.

I am grateful for my loving sister and two brothers, who all helped me find my way.

And finally I thank John Bucklin for his photograph on the book cover. My heart is overflowing with gratitude for my family who surround me with their love.

ALSO BY LINDA HALE BUCKLIN

The Love of Angels

Beyond His Control

Come Rain or Come Shine

ABOUT THE AUTHOR

A fourth generation San Franciscan, Linda Bucklin has worked in public relations and as a freelance writer. Her articles have appeared in *House & Garden, Journal of Commerce*, and *Nob Hill Gazette*. She now lives in Mill Valley and feels blessed to be surrounded by her three sons, two daughters-in-law, and four grandchildren.

With Mary Keil, she wrote *Come Rain or Come Shine* (Adams Press, 1999), a book about women's friendships. More recently she received accolades for *Beyond His Control* (ePublishing Works, 2008), her memoir about growing up in a privileged family that was shattered with the suicide of her beloved mother. The book went on to become a *New York Times* best-seller in paperback and e-book editions.

The Love of Angels (ePublishing Works, 2016), her third book, a collection of stories, including the author's own, chronicles encounters with angels, spiritual beings, and living people who show up to remind us of love's power. Her fourth book, *The Distant Shore* was written after the loss of her husband in 2016. Through her own stories and others' enlightening experiences, she explores the possibility of life after death.

Linda served for many years as a trustee of Grace Cathedral. A nationally ranked tennis player, she became #1 in the U.S. in 60's mixed doubles with her long-time partner Charlie Hoeveler in 2006. Linda now holds six national titles. In addition to her family and friends, her other passions include duplicate bridge (she recently became a Life Master), fly-fishing, and camping under the star-studded Montana sky.